# SIMPLE
# PAINTED
# FURNITURE

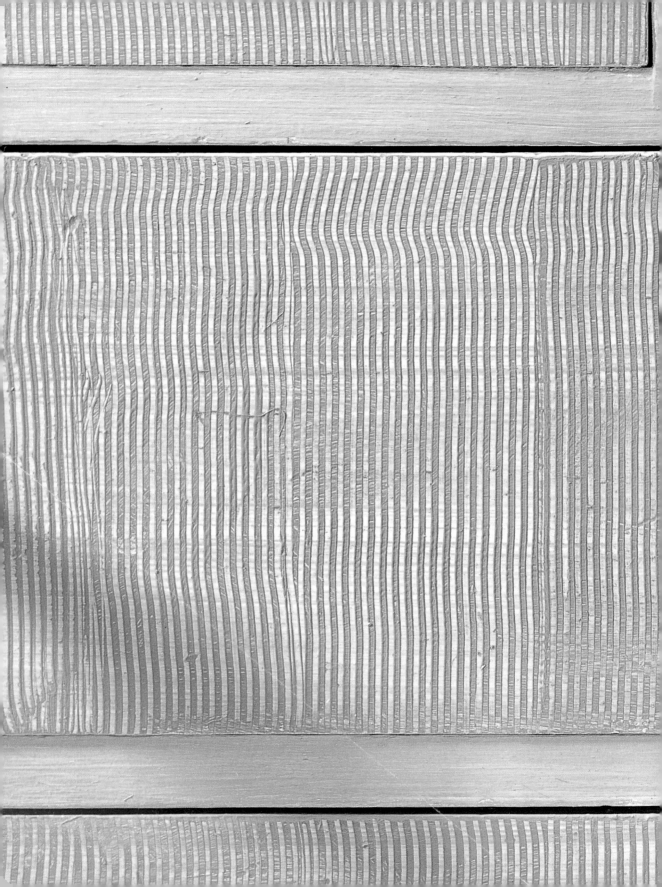

# SIMPLE
# PAINTED
# FURNITURE

## ANNIE SLOAN

PHOTOGRAPHS BY
DAVID MURRAY AND MICHAEL MURRAY

DORLING KINDERSLEY
LONDON

*TO MY MOTHER, DOLORES*

Editor Christiane Gunzi

Designed by Peter Bridgewater,
Bridgewater Design Limited

Editorial Director Amy Carroll
Senior Managing Art Editor Denise Brown

Production Henrietta Winthrop

First Published in Great Britain in 1989 by
Dorling Kindersley Limited, 9 Henrietta Street, London WC2 8PS
First paperback edition 1991

Reprinted in 1994

Sloan, Annie
Simple painted furniture.
1. Furniture. Painting. Amateurs: annuals
I. Title
749
ISBN 0-86318-759-5

Typeset in England by CST
Reproduced in Singapore by Colourscan
Printed and bound in Spain by Graficromo

# CONTENTS

# INTRODUCTION

I first became aware of painted furniture sixteen years ago, when I read a book called *The Flowering of American Folk Art*, by Jean Lipman and Alice Winchester. It was there that I first saw and marvelled at the highly imaginative painted furniture made by the first European settlers in America. Later on, and many books later, I had a wealth of decorative styles and techniques with which to inspire myself to do some practical experiments of my own.

The history of painted furniture in Europe began with the opening-up of trade routes to the East by the Dutch, and their introduction to the ancient art of lacquerwork. By the seventeenth century, small items of lacquerwork were being imported in other parts of Europe, too. Oriental lacquerwork proved so popular that demand soon outweighed production, which was slow and painstaking. The art was soon copied by European furniture-makers, developing into *chinoiserie*, a style of decoration based on Chinese motifs. Each country developed its own method, using different varnishes, glues and pigments, until a Western style of painted furniture emerged.

Another early influence on the art of painted furniture in Europe, apparent before the fashion for *chinoiserie*, was Northern European folk art, or peasant painting. This was particularly abundant in Sweden, Bavaria and Switzerland, where wooden furniture was hand-painted to relieve the monotony of the readily available bare wood. Such European decorative painting

**Storing materials and equipment**
*An old drawer is ideal for storing all your tubes of paints, pens and pencils in. I keep much of my equipment in this old kitchen drawer. The addition of a few slats of wood, to serve as dividers, helps to keep everything neat and tidy.*

was taken to America by Scandinavian and German emigrants, and there developed into a style known as Pennsylvania Dutch. As interesting wood became scarce and more expensive in the nineteenth century, painted *papier mâché* became extremely popular in Europe, as painted furniture became less so.

Today, it is once again fashionable for furniture to be painted. The plethora of pine pieces, which are readily available second-hand, and new, has encouraged people to try their hands at personalising their furniture to add a certain individuality. I hope this book will encourage others to produce their own painted furniture, either using one of the traditional styles, or experimenting with a fresh, innovational approach.

## CHOOSING SOMETHING TO DECORATE

The greatest joy in preparing this book has been in transforming furniture that nobody else wanted into something of interest. I scoured junk shops and furniture emporiums, and accepted old unwanted items from friends, in my search for paintable furniture. Secondhand furniture shops are usually stuffed full of cheaply made mass-produced pieces. These are solidly made and veneered, and once the shiny varnish has been removed from the veneer, they are ideal for painting. Oak is a solid wood which is often more reasonably priced than the more popular pine, although pine can still be bought cheaply if you are willing to repair any areas that have been damaged.

**Restoring old paintbrushes**
Good quality household brushes can
last for years if you look after them
well. To bring old, shabby brushes
back to life, try soaking them in
brush restorer.

In choosing a piece of furniture to decorate, I always look for something with an interesting or unusual shape. I soon learned to ignore dark varnishes because they can be removed, and ugly handles, because they can be replaced.

### PAINTING FURNITURE

A place to work in is the first consideration. For most people, painting a piece of furniture means making a temporary space on the kitchen table or floor. I therefore recommend using acrylic paint rather than oil colour, because it dries quickly, and is less messy, so cleaning your brushes is easier. I have painted most of the furniture with oil colour, but many of the pieces lend themselves to acrylic paint.

I had great fun choosing how to paint my pieces of furniture, since the choice of style and colour is immense. Some pieces immediately sparked off a stream of different ideas, while others dictated exactly the one technique I should use. For the basecoats, I chose eggshell paint because the surface has a slight sheen which is not too glossy, and the hard-wearing finish is ideal for chairs and tables. If you prefer, use emulsion paint, which is water-based and dries quickly, but bear in mind that oil work cannot be done on top of it.

Throughout the book, I often refer to "off-white" eggshell. This is a name of my own, rather than the name of a specific colour. There are dozens of off-white colours available, and, while some names change, according to fashions of the time, a few, such as magnolia and gardenia remain year after year.

On most of the furniture, I have used clear mid-sheen polyurethane varnish to seal and protect the painted surface, but you could use a matt or gloss finish instead. When buying varnish, always ask for a clear, non-yellowing varnish. None are absolutely transparent, but a few good-quality varnishes come close. Lastly, before you do any painting of your own, refer to my list of useful tips.

## ANNIE'S TIPS

♦ When choosing something to paint, check that it is made of real wood, and not plywood. Beware of woodworm, and also thick layers of paint, which take hours to remove.

♦ Prepare your surface well before painting; fill holes, then sand and seal the surface until it is ready for the basecoat. Protect surrounding areas with old sheets.

♦ Ventilation in the room where you work is of paramount importance. Paint stripper, white spirit and glaze are highly inflammable, so never smoke, or use a fan heater where you are working, and always open the windows.

♦ If you wear gloves while working with white spirit or brush cleaner, use PVC or vinyl gloves, rather than natural rubber or polythene ones, which absorb the vapours.

♦ Aim for the smoothest surface possible when applying the basecoat, sanding with wet and dry sandpaper if necessary, and allow each layer of paint to dry thoroughly.

♦ When painting a table or chair, always turn the piece upside-down and paint the legs first.

♦ Apply tinted glazes and other paint layers very thinly to avoid a build-up of paint.

♦ Note that clear glaze, also called transparent oil glaze, does not look clear in the can – it is off-white or honey-coloured.

♦ Finally, if you are in any doubt about the difference between eggshell and emulsion, tinted glaze and clear glaze, oil colour and acrylic paint, simply refer to The Glossary of Painting Terms on p.92 for help.

*Throughout the book, the initial letters of standardized artists' colours are in upper case (e.g. Raw Sienna and Burnt Umber); other colour names, such as poppy red and off-white are purely descriptive.*

# THE PAINTED FURNITURE

# STIPPLED CORNER CUPBOARD

I TOOK A RISK when I bought this cupboard, thinking that I could transform it into a beautiful piece of furniture. It looked so hideous when I first saw it, that I was tempted not to buy it at all. The cupboard, which is Victorian, originally had large ornate shelves with mirrors underneath, and when I took it home, the first thing I did was to take it apart very carefully; this is the top section. I also discovered that it had been ebonized (painted black), and some time later, painted white. I thought it wise to make certain it was not of antique value before I started to decorate it. Both a furniture specialist, and a friend of mine who deals in antiques, told me that the cupboard was beyond restoration, so I began to set about giving it a new lease of life, and wondered what sort of finish would suit the cupboard best.

For inspiration, I had in my workshop a small antique gilt-edged cabinet that needed restoring. Although it seemed rather grand to me in its appearance, the same dealer who had pronounced the Victorian cupboard to have no antique value, had referred to the cabinet as being "country-style". I decided to reproduce a similar gilt-edged "country-style" look on my corner cupboard. I was amused by the cupboard's pretensions, so, in keeping with the station it aspired to, I created the look of a rich damask or brocade interior, by printing on some stuck-on calico and lining the edges with braiding. I stippled the exterior of the cupboard in a deep green, traditional of the eighteenth century, then added wax gilt detailing along the edges to complete the look.

**Printing with polystyrene**
*For the printed pattern on the interior of the corner cupboard, I used a printing block made out of a piece of polystyrene packing-case. I chose to print a traditional design because it was so in keeping with the Victorian style of the cupboard.*

*Many different designs can be created with a little imagination, and the most simple shapes are often the most effective. When making a printing block, always experiment first, by printing with it on a piece of paper to see how the design looks.*

**White spirit** to add to the clear glaze and oil colour

**Cream-coloured eggshell** for the basecoat

**Clear glaze**

**Cotton rag**

**Clear mid-sheen polyurethane varnish,** which can be tinted with a little oil colour, to seal and protect the surface of the calico

**Oxide of Chromium, Venetian Red** and **Monestial Green oil colour** to use with a stippling brush on the exterior

**Stippling brush** for the main part of the cupboard

**Off-white emulsion** to mix with green acrylic paint for the interior

**Glue** for sticking down the fabric

**Calico** for the interior, with a scalpel for trimming, and Oxide of Chromium and Emerald Green oil colour for the printing

**Polystyrene blocks** for printing the pattern inside the cupboard, with a bristle brush for applying the colour to the blocks

**Painted braid** with rub-on wax gilt cream

## METHOD

◆ First apply your chosen basecoat and leave it to dry.

◆ Over this, paint on a tinted glaze close in tone to the basecoat, and stipple it. Allow the stippled glaze to dry thoroughly.

◆ If you are making a printed interior, cut out and stick down a piece of calico shaped to fit. Cover it with a basecoat that tones in well with the other paintwork.

◆ Cut out your printing block(s). Polystyrene is particularly good to use because the glaze does not soak in too quickly. Print the design(s) in an irregular way in your chosen colours. Allow to dry.

◆ Coat the dry surface with a thin layer of clear mid-sheen polyurethane varnish, into which a little oil colour of the appropriate tone has been added. This will seal the surface, and bring in the background colour to make the composition look complete.

◆ Along any raised, carved, moulded, or other suitable edges, apply a little rub-on wax gilt cream with your finger. This will make the surface appear gilded, thus highlighting the edges.

◆ If you wish, glue some braid in a matching tone along the edges in order to hide the joins.

The interior of this cupboard was very ugly, being covered in a modern raised wallpaper and painted a wishy-washy pale blue. It proved very difficult to remove and, in addition, the wood underneath was of poor quality. I began to wonder if the interior had originally been fabric, so I bought some calico, cut it to fit and glued it on. I overlapped the edges of the fabric and used a sharp scalpel to cut off the excess.

When this was dry, I painted it with water-based paint for quickness of drying, using a mixture of off-white emulsion and Oxide of Chromium and Monestial Green acrylic. Rather than having to buy expensive cloth, I was able to reproduce a damask pattern that was in keeping with the style of the cupboard. I made a printing block from a piece of polystyrene found in a packing case, cutting out two patterns reminiscent of damask, and printed the calico in darker tones than the basecoat.

Since I could not buy braiding to match the colours of the cupboard, I painted the braid, then rubbed a little wax gilt cream over it to echo the gilt edging on the cupboard.

# TROMPE L'OEIL TABLE

THIS TABLE IS THE most simple, in some ways, of all the pieces I have painted. I took a plain, ordinary table with no redeeming features and of no particular colour, and transformed it into a surprisingly pretty breakfast table. The technique of *trompe l'oeil* ("deceives the eye") paint-ing can look charming, but, as the French name suggests, it is sometimes rather ostentatious, and at its worst, laborious and overworked. I have always liked *trompe l'oeil* effects best when their themes are simple. At first glance, the role of the *trompe l'oeil* is to deceive the eye into believing that it is seeing something three-dimensional, rather than a flat painted surface. To achieve this, your subject-matter must always be painted whole and life-size, since the illusion is not convincing if objects are reduced or enlarged, or cut off at the edges as in a photograph. The *trompe l'oeil* object must also fit realistically into its setting in order for it to be credible.

Complicated *trompe l'oeil* painting is quite difficult to do well, but if you choose a straightforward theme to begin with, for example a table-cloth, the effect is simple, yet at the same time extremely effective. I like this table best when the flaps are down, revealing that it is just a painted table-cloth. This idea could be treated in a number of ways, an alternative approach being to paint an elaborate red and white gingham table-cloth, or one with a border of "embroidered" flowers. For my breakfast table, I was thinking of a simple cotton cloth like those found in many homes today, which would go well with my blue farmhouse crockery.

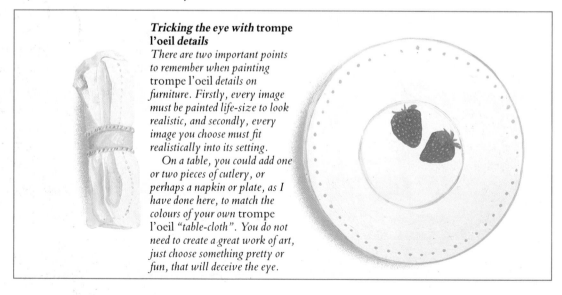

### Tricking the eye with trompe l'oeil *details*

*There are two important points to remember when painting* trompe l'oeil *details on furniture. Firstly, every image must be painted life-size to look realistic, and secondly, every image you choose must fit realistically into its setting.*

*On a table, you could add one or two pieces of cutlery, or perhaps a napkin or plate, as I have done here, to match the colours of your own* trompe l'oeil *"table-cloth". You do not need to create a great work of art, just choose something pretty or fun, that will deceive the eye.*

**Cream-coloured eggshell** *for the basecoat*

**Household brush** *for applying the basecoat*

**Clear mid-sheen polyurethane varnish** *to seal and protect the surface of the table top*

**Small artist's brush** *to use for the lining*

**Ruler** *to use for the lining on the "table-cloth"*

**Masking tape** *for marking off the area to be painted*

**Cobalt Blue** *oil colour to mix with the cream-coloured eggshell*

---

## METHOD

♦ Mask off around the area that you wish to paint, using masking tape and paper too, if necessary. To paint the shape of a table-cloth, always mask off the corners of the table first.

♦ Apply your chosen basecoat, and allow it to dry thoroughly. Eggshell paint is particularly suitable for table tops because it gives a hard-wearing finish. It produces a surface that is not too shiny, therefore it is much more appropriate than gloss paint

for simulating cloth. You may need to apply several coats, until you achieve the depth of colour that you require. For a really smooth surface, sand in between the basecoat layers.

♦ To add lines to your "table-cloth", use a ruler, a small brush and preferably, oil-based paint, so that you can wipe off any mistakes.

♦ Add other *trompe l'oeil* details if you wish, taking care to choose images that

will look realistic when painted on your piece of furniture. The images must be painted life-size in order for them to be credible.

♦ Leave the painted surface to dry, then apply one or more coats of clear mid-sheen polyurethane varnish. If your "table-cloth" is white, apply only one coat of varnish (thinned with white spirit) to retain the brightness of the white paintwork. Give the unpainted areas several coats of varnish.

Before painting the table, I marked off a square shape with masking tape, as if the table had been laid with a plain square table-cloth, the corner of which just hung over the sides. I chose eggshell paint because it is tough and would not need to be varnished afterwards. I painted inside the masked-off area with cream-coloured eggshell, but on removing the masking tape, I found that the edges looked much too sharp. To counter this, I applied the next two coats of eggshell in freehand without masking tape, to give the edges a soft, undefined look, as if they were made of real fabric. When this had dried, I took a ruler and a bristle brush, and added lines in a mixture of light blue eggshell and Cobalt Blue oil colour, which I pulled along the side of the ruler to make the blue lines. I used eggshell with the oil colour because it adds depth to the colour without too much shine, while the oil colour gives brightness of tone.

Finally, I protected the surface with clear mid-sheen polyurethane varnish to provide a hard-wearing surface. To retain the whiteness of the cloth, I applied only one coat of varnish.

# PRINTED SEMI-CIRCULAR TABLE

THIS SEMI-CIRCULAR TABLE that was bought by a friend from a junk shop, seemed ideal for some decorative paintwork. Although I knew it was not a valuable antique, I found its delicate shape extremely elegant. In the past, such a side table would have filled the corner of a hallway or dining room, and, even today, it is a handy-shaped item where space is limited.

The design and colours that I chose for the decoration were influenced by a little table I had seen in a Paris museum. That rather rustic eighteenth-century table is painted with the fresh, summery colours of cornflower blue and cream, and the top is shaped like a tray, so perhaps originally it would have been used for afternoon tea. I particularly liked the table's curved legs, which has feet shaped like goats' hooves. Perhaps it was made by a French artisan, who had worked in a big country house or château and, having seen the beautiful blue and white porcelain being imported into Europe in vast quantities at that time, had been inspired to paint the table in a similar way.

Although I was sure of my colour scheme of blue and cream, I was a little uncertain of my design for this piece, so I needed a flexible technique. For this reason, I chose eggshell paint for the basecoat, and oil colour for the decoration. As these paints are slow-drying, this meant that I could alter my design as I went along until I was happy with it. I wanted to paint the table with a design that incorporated classical shapes, but I also wanted the paintwork to have a slightly distressed look, as though roughened by age. Therefore, instead of using brushes, I thought about using a method of printing that would produce slightly imperfect, yet regular shapes, which is important when you are doing a repeating pattern. In the end, I used pieces of corrugated card to make the arabesque and honey-comb shapes, and the lid of the paint can and a makeshift compass to produce the more rigid circular shapes. Before printing, I painted the table with a slightly distressed cream colour that set off the Prussian Blue images beautifully – my homage to the classical French furniture of the eighteenth century.

### Making printed effects with card

*The elaborate designs on the table were made simply by printing the surface with torn-up strips of corrugated card dipped in oil colour.*

*The three examples shown here illustrate how simple it is to produce several different effects with just a few suitable pieces of torn-up packing- case.*

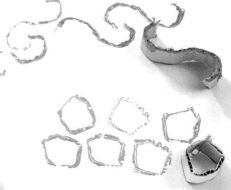

**Wet and dry sandpaper** to smooth down the basecoat layers once they have dried

**Cream-coloured** eggshell basecoat

**Cotton rag** for wiping off the excess glaze

**Clear mid-sheen polyurethane varnish,** to tint with oil colour for an antique finish

**Household brush** for applying the eggshell basecoat

**Cobalt Blue and Burnt Umber oil colour** and cream-coloured eggshell applied with an artist's brush to produce the Prussian Blue colour

**Small pieces of corrugated card** to be dipped into the colour to print the arabesque and honeycomb shapes

**Some household string, with a pencil** attached to one end, and a drawing pin in the centre – to use as a makeshift compass for drawing large semi-circles around the table top

**Coarse wire wool,** to rub away the lumps and bumps on the painted surface, and to take away the newness of the paintwork, to produce an antique look

## METHOD

◆ Paint on your chosen basecoat. Allow it to dry, then rub it over with wet and dry sandpaper. Follow with a second coat of the basecoat colour, repeat the sanding, and apply a third coat. When dry, rub over the final coat with wet and dry sandpaper once more for a really smooth finish.

◆ If your piece has any moulding or carved detailing, take some oil colour (Raw Umber is a good choice) and, using an artist's brush, rub the colour into the holes and over the ridges.

◆ After about five minutes, while the surface is tacky, wipe the edges with a rag, removing some colour to produce a distressed look. If you wish, continue to paint and wipe to give the edges an interesting finish.

◆ To add semi-circular lines to your furniture, find the centre point along the back edge. Take a piece of string of the appropriate length, and attach a pencil to one end and a drawing-pin to the other. Secure the pin in the centre-back of the flat edge and pull the pencil and string around in a semi-circle. You can paint over this line with an artist's brush.

◆ Complete the design, using pieces of card, a stencil or freehand painting.

◆ Once the surface is dry, rub it with coarse wire wool to take away the newness. Apply tinted mid-sheen polyurethane varnish.

When I was given this table, it had been painted in white gloss paint over varnish, which was not a good surface to paint on since it chips quite readily. However, this meant that I could peel the paint off easily, which I did in about four hours. The next stage was to apply some stripper and, using a scraper, I removed most of the varnish. On the legs and moulded edge, I used small pieces of coarse wire wool soaked in white spirit to get into the corners.

Once the surface was dry, I applied three coats of the cream-coloured eggshell basecoat, and rubbed the Prussian Blue mixture on to the carved moulded trim. For the arabesque design, I took a brown cardboard packing-case (with corrugated card on the inside), tore off several strips of 2- to 3-inch pieces and applied paint to their edges. With these, I printed lines which were sometimes straight and sometimes curved. Once the printing was dry, I rubbed the table all over with coarse wire wool to take the new-ness and any lumps of paint away, rubbing away some areas almost completely to give the piece an antique look.

Lastly, I applied a coat of clear mid-sheen polyurethane varnish, tinted with Cobalt Blue and Burnt Umber oil colour and cream-coloured eggshell; this "dirtied" the varnish, contributing to the aged look of the table.

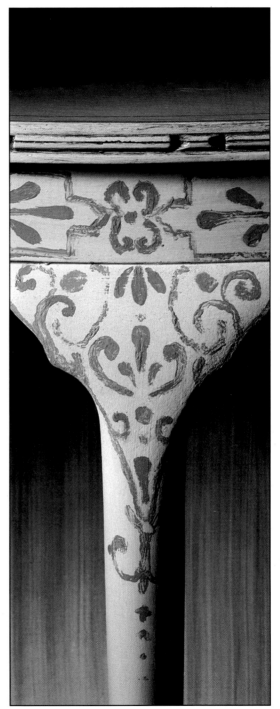

▲ I drew the curved lines with a pencil on a stretched length of string. On smaller items, you could draw around a paint can or a dinner plate.

▶ For the decorative curled and straight arabesque shapes, I printed with strips of card, and used the tip of my brush for the dots and petal shapes.

# POTATO-PRINTED MIRROR FRAME

THE DECORATIVE treatment of this mirror was inspired by a picture frame that I saw in the Italian home of some friends about a year ago, and the choice of colour and pattern is based on my memory of that lovely piece. I had slight misgivings about the mirror frame when I bought it, because I disliked its dark heavy varnish, but I felt certain that it would look much more attractive painted in a paler colour. The mirror was originally supposed to hang as a square, but it looked so heavy with its big circles at the corners, that I moved the chain to make it diamond-shaped.

As a background for printing, my alternate painting and wiping with a dry rag produced a subtle, but effective limed look. Into the awkward corners and carved moulding, I pushed a brush loaded with paint, then wiped a damp sponge over them to ensure that the paint covered everywhere. I removed any excess paint from the frame with a clean cotton rag before the paint had time to dry.

I knew that by adding potato prints to my painted surface, I could echo and enhance the shape of the mirror frame by using repeated geometric shapes. Printing with potatoes, and other vegetable printing blocks, is particularly rewarding, as the resulting delicate, simple and slightly imperfect prints are charming. Vegetables are both easy and cheap to print with, and there is almost always a potato in the larder! Although many people consider potato-printing to produce a naive, childish effect, a sophisticated look can be achieved too, if you cut out the shape of the printing block absolutely evenly then load it carefully with paint. Rectangular shapes can be made easily too, simply by printing with the side of an old eraser.

**Experimenting with printed shapes**

*The diamond shapes printed on the mirror frame were extremely easy to do. With half a potato, or a piece of carrot, and a sharp knife, you can create all sorts of patterns. Experiment with corks, old erasers and other objects too, trying out patterns and colours until you find a suitable design.*

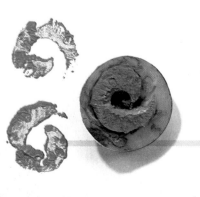

**Off-white emulsion** to paint and wipe over the mirror frame with a rag

**Paper and masking tape** to protect the mirror glass

**Piece of wood** on which the colours are mixed

**Sponge and water** for wiping off excess colour

**Potatoes and eraser** to print with, and a vegetable knife for cutting out the printing blocks

**Hoghair fitch** for painting the raised edges and inner mouldings

**Oxide of Chromium, French Ultramarine, Payne's Grey and Titanium White acrylic paint** for painting and printing

---

## METHOD

♦ Always mask off the glass on mirrors to avoid splashes, then apply your chosen basecoat to the frame, and leave it to dry.

♦ If you wish, paint and wipe the surface to add interest. Do this by applying a thinned layer of oil- or water-based paint to the frame, then wipe it off with a rag or cloth before it dries. You may need to do this twice before you are satisfied with the effect. If the result looks too heavy, simply wipe it off with a damp sponge or cotton rag.

♦ While it is still wet, wipe the colour over any raised, carved or moulded areas with a clean rag or sponge, then add highlights to these edges in a paler tone, using the side of a bristle brush. Wipe off any excess paint with a clean rag or sponge and leave to dry.

♦ Take a potato half or other suitable vegetable and cut out your shape; make certain that the shape is equally balanced and that it stands about ¼-inch proud of the surface.

♦ Brush your chosen colour on to the printing block and press it over the surface, wherever you wish. If using acrylic paint, remember that it dries more quickly than oil colour, and slightly darker in tone. If you prefer, print with an old eraser or a cork instead. To produce more texture and interest, print over the shapes for a second time in a lighter tone.

♦ It is not necessary to protect a frame with any varnish.

*Whereas on some items I like to add wax gilt to the carved moulding as an extra detail, I chose to leave this moulding plain so that the simple diamond shapes would be the main feature.*

*Carved moulding can look extremely effective with gilt added, but gilt can also overload a simple painted finish such as this one. Here, the beading provides enough interest.*

First of all, I protected the mirror glass with masking tape and paper, then used varnish remover on the dark oak frame to bleach it a little and reduce the heaviness. Three coats of bleach made little difference, so I lightened the wood with off-white emulsion. I could picture the effect that I wanted to achieve, but the white paintwork left the mirror looking rather stark. Eventually, the effect was softened successfully with a mixture of French Ultramarine and Payne's Grey acrylic paint. I wiped this over the mirror, left it to dry, then added highlights using Oxide of Chromium, Payne's Grey and Titanium White. For the potato-printing, I used Oxide of Chromium, French Ultramarine, Payne's Grey and Titanium White.

# GILT-STENCILLED TABLE

SMALL OCCASIONAL TABLES SUCH as this one are often seen in old furniture shops in some shape or form, and are generally not well made. This one, however, was a better shape than usual, and although in bad condition, it was quite solidly made. Having just bought some rub-on wax gilt cream that I was keen to experiment with, I began to imagine how rich and ornate the table could look, stencilled with some gilding. The slightly scalloped edges conjured up images of ebonized Victorian furniture, and I was filled with enthusiasm as I planned the decoration. A book of Victorian stencils that I had at home contained exactly the sort of highly-decorative design that I wanted. There is quite a range of stencil books available, so you can find all kinds of subject-matter.

My final design used two of the most ornate stencils; one in the centre of the table, with the other one repeated around the edge. I used part of the large stencil to fill in the empty spaces on the underside of the table. Gilding on its own can look too bright and gaudy, and a richer effect is achieved by applying it over gesso. The gilding does not have to cover the gesso completely; allowing some of the redness to show through by shifting the stencil slightly off-centre is often much more interesting. This rich combination of red and gold on black enhanced the table to such an extent that it now blends in beautifully with its setting.

**Choosing your designs**
The elaborate Victorian-style design on the table top was made using some stencils from a book of Victorian stencil designs. The six examples shown here are also taken from that book. Each of the designs could look effective on its own, or in conjunction with another design.

There are many books of cut-out stencils available, which contain quite a variety of subject-matter, but it is also simple to make your own stencils, using stencil card, manila paper or acetate.

**Black eggshell basecoat**

**Clear mid-sheen polyurethane varnish** *to seal the table and give it a shiny finish*

**Household brush** *for applying the basecoat*

**Ready-made red gesso to use with** *the stencil to produce the red base*

**Small bristle brush and stencil brush** *for adding the gesso and gilding*

**Stencils,** *of two different types, from a book of Victorian designs*

**Rub-on wax gilt cream** *to apply over the gesso*

**Craft knife and spray adhesive** *for cutting the stencils and keeping them in place*

♦ Apply your chosen basecoat and allow it to dry thoroughly.

♦ Make your stencil(s) from stencil paper, oiled manila paper or acetate, or, if you prefer, cut out a design from a stencil book.

♦ Position the stencil(s), on your surface, using masking tape or a little spray adhesive. In this way, they can then be repositioned easily.

♦ Apply ready-made coloured gesso to the stencil, using a small brush or your finger. If you prefer, use oil colour or acrylic paint, letting it dry completely before adding any wax gilt cream to the surface.

♦ When the surface is dry, apply rub-on wax gilt cream through the stencil (positioned slightly off-centre, if you wish the gesso to show through), rubbing the gilt on with your finger. Rub-on wax gilt cream is available in various tones of gold, some are quite yellow, others more red.

♦ To protect the stencilled surface, apply one or more coats of clear mid-sheen polyurethane varnish.

This table was riddled with woodworm, which I treated, then filled the holes with wax filler, and rubbed the surface smooth with wire wool.

I painted the table with black eggshell, and when it was dry, positioned my stencils, and applied ready-made red gesso with a brush. I also applied gesso to the edges, then brushed on some wax gilt cream, removing the excess with my finger. Finally, I applied a coat of clear mid-sheen polyurethane varnish.

# DRAGGED HALL CUPBOARD

 I WAS IMMEDIATELY ATTRACTED to this tall oak wardrobe, with its extraordinary arched panels and the curious curtain. Its rather Gothic appearance was also suggestive of the Arts and Crafts Movement to a certain extent, and I felt quite enthusiastic about its decorative potential. Once home, however, I looked more closely at the wardrobe, and for a while, I was not so sure that I liked it after all. The glass bull's-eye pane that I had not taken much notice of before now looked ugly and sham. The cupboard began to remind me of a strange sort of confessional box, probably because of its shape and the little curtain. To add to the aura of the Gothic, the door was stuck fast, and I began to wonder what I might find inside. The handle was broken, so I had to prise the door open with a screwdriver, where I found nothing but an old key.

I decided to drag the cupboard in a light colour to brighten it and to incorporate it into its twentieth-century surroundings. The dragging also seemed to enhance its general shape, and the greeny-blue colour somehow evoked a sense of the Arts and Crafts Movement, yet at the same time looked quite modern too.

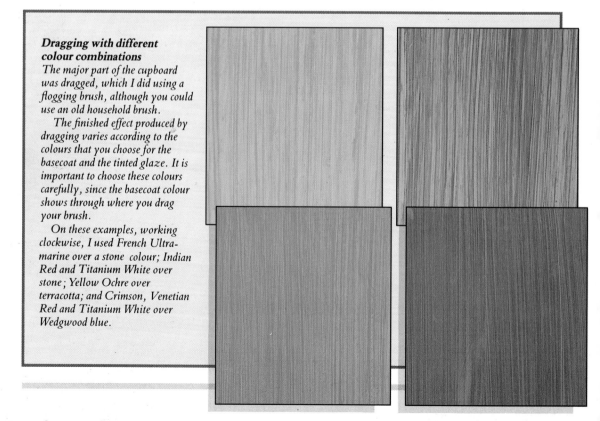

**Dragging with different colour combinations**
The major part of the cupboard was dragged, which I did using a flogging brush, although you could use an old household brush.

The finished effect produced by dragging varies according to the colours that you choose for the basecoat and the tinted glaze. It is important to choose these colours carefully, since the basecoat colour shows through where you drag your brush.

On these examples, working clockwise, I used French Ultramarine over a stone colour; Indian Red and Titanium White over stone; Yellow Ochre over terracotta; and Crimson, Venetian Red and Titanium White over Wedgwood blue.

**White spirit** to mix with oil colour and eggshell paint

**Clear glaze** to mix with white spirit, off-white eggshell and oil colour for the dragging

**Raw Umber, Monestial Green and Prussian Blue oil colour,** to mix together in unequal amounts with white spirit and off-white eggshell, to produce the pale blue colour for the dragging

**Jam jar** containing a mixture of Raw Umber, Prussian Blue and Monestial Green oil colour with off-white eggshell for the basecoat, with an old brush to mix the colours

**Flogging brush** for the dragging, with a household brush for the basecoat

**Mutton cloth** for wiping over the panelled and carved areas, to contrast with the dragging

## METHOD

◆ Apply your chosen basecoat and allow it to dry. Always mask off any areas of glass on your furniture, using masking tape, and paper too, if necessary, before you begin to paint.

◆ Prepare a tinted glaze, and drag the piece, applying the tinted glaze very thinly with a flogging brush or a coarse, dry household brush. Always keep the colours of the basecoat and the tinted glaze close in tone.

◆ If you wish, wipe a mutton cloth over panelled, moulded or carved areas to add interest, and dab off some areas of colour to produce a slightly cloudy look, to contrast with the dragging. Alternatively, ragging would also complement the dragged areas well.

◆ Once dry, apply one or more coats of clear mid-sheen polyurethane varnish to protect the surface.

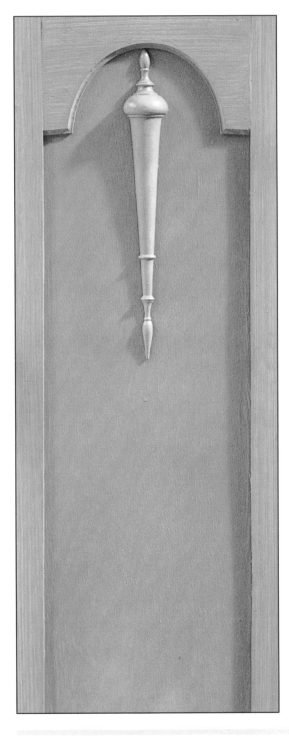

I cleaned the cupboard first with wax cleaner to remove all the old wax and dirt, then keyed the surface by rubbing it all over with coarse wire wool. Next, I applied a cream-coloured base-coat to lighten it, as I thought it was a little large and dark. Somehow it seemed to lose its character at this stage, and obviously needed to be reasonably strong in colour. I decided to use a grey-blue colour, which immediately livened up the surface and added interest.

For the dragging, I used the same mixture of colours in a lighter tone than the basecoat. I made a tinted glaze, using off-white eggshell and Raw Umber oil colour, with a little Prussian Blue and Monestial Green. This I applied thinly, and dragged it a number of times with a flogging brush to get a broken grain effect. This could be done with a coarse, dry household brush, but a flogging brush produces a wide-grained effect more easily. I applied a darker tinted glaze to the arch-shaped panels, then wiped them with a mutton cloth. To complete the effect, I added a new copper-look door handle to replace the old broken one.

◀ *After dragging the main part of the cupboard, I decided to make a feature of the panelled areas, and the unusual carving. To highlight the long pieces of carving, I simply wiped over them with my mutton-cloth.*

▲ *I liked the colour of the original curtain in the window of the cupboard, and decided not to replace it with a new curtain. The deep mustard colour contrasts well with the greeny-grey tones of the painted wood.*

# WOOD-FINISH BEDSTEAD

THIS SINGLE BED, WITH high headboards and footboards, is one of a pair that I bought because they looked so unusual, but it is probably not all that old, judging by the style of the medallion on the headboard. When I bought the two beds, this one was in good condition and really only needed a clean, while the other bed was damaged, and is still waiting to be repaired. I wondered what sort of finish would look best on this type of bed – the large expanse of headboard seemed to invite a mock wood effect of some kind. I considered the different alternatives, and since the room I intended to keep it in had sunny yellow walls, I finally chose a maple-like wood effect, which I knew would tone in beautifully with the colour scheme of this cheery little room. It is important, when attempting to simulate the look of real wood, that you spend time studying its colour and grain, in order for the painted results to be as realistic as possible.

The tradition of painted bedsteads probably owes much to the shape of Northern European beds, whose large, flat, bare expanses of wood provided the perfect surface for decorative painting. Painted bedroom furniture was particularly abundant in Bavaria during the seventeenth century, and its popularity soon spread to Holland, Switzerland and Scandinavia. Since wood was cheap and readily available, and the winters extremely cold, a distinctive high-sided, built-in style of bed developed which was particularly popular in peasant houses. The shape of beds such as mine most certainly relates to those high-sided wooden beds.

*Choosing suitable colours*

*For the wood-finish bedstead, I chose a simple maple wood effect, which tones in well with my yellow room. The colour and tonal quality of the tinted glaze(s) are most important when you are woodgraining, and you should study a real piece of wood first, in order to mix appropriate glazes. The basecoat should match the lightest colour of the real wood, and the tinted glaze(s), the darker tones.*

*In these examples, I used French Ultramarine and Burnt Umber over a blue-grey basecoat for the grey "wood", and for the golden-brown example I used several tones of Raw Sienna and Titanium White.*

**Clear glaze and white spirit** *for the tinted glaze mixture, with a household brush*

**Basecoat** *mixed in a jam jar, using off-white eggshell, donkey-brown eggshell and a little Yellow Ochre oil colour*

**Paint tray with Yellow Ochre, Burnt Umber and Burnt Sienna oil colour** *for the tinted glaze*

**Clean cotton rag** *with a household brush and softening brush*

**Ivory Black oil colour** *and a swordliner for the lining*

**Clear mid-sheen polyurethane varnish** *to protect the surface*

## METHOD

♦ Apply the basecoat of your choice, matching it to the lightest colour of the wood that you are imitating.

♦ Prepare a tinted glaze to match the darker tone of the wood, keeping the mixture quite runny, and close in tone to the basecoat.

♦ Apply the tinted glaze with a household brush, pressing it down at regular intervals to release the colour for the darker areas. For small items, apply the tinted glaze, then brush over it with a wiggling movement in an irregular way, pressing the brush down to release more tinted glaze.

♦ While the surface is tacky, go over it with a softening brush to blend the tones slightly, testing a small area first, to see how wet it is.

♦ If you wish, add thin lines to certain areas, such as carved mouldings or rims, to add definition. Use oil colour and a swordliner. Leave it to dry.

♦ Apply one or two coats of clear mid-sheen polyurethane varnish to protect the surface.

In order to do the wood finish, I took the bed apart completely, and I painted each section flat on a table. This made the work much easier because the consistency of the tinted glaze was thin, and I wanted to avoid making drips.

It does not matter in which order you paint the separate pieces of a bed, but it is important to allow each surface to dry thoroughly before painting its reverse side. I chose to paint the sides first, until I felt proficient enough to start on the headboard. At this stage, the effect looks a little crude, but if you wait a while to let the white spirit evaporate, the tinted glaze is left looking oily-wet, but not runny. The surface can then be brushed with a softening brush to blend all the tones.

*To add a little definition to the carved areas on the head- and footboard, I dragged my brush horizontally across the oval medallion shape, which produced a rich, golden grainy effect – rather like tiger's eye. The slightly different finish on these carved areas provides a subtle, but effective contrast with the rest of the bed.*

# RAGGED, LINED TABLE

THIS LITTLE TABLE did not look particularly exciting when I bought it, but its simplicity appealed to me, and I found it endearing. It was plain oak, and the grain of the wood was not interesting, but I knew it would look quite pretty and jolly with a little work. I ragged the table top, which suited the main part of the piece, giving it a more robust look, and dragged its delicately tapering legs. This, together with the lining around the top added elegance to what was originally quite an ordinary little table. It now looked bright and cheerful, but also needed some sort of detailing to provide a contrast with the blue paintwork.

After some consideration, I chose to paint a flower motif on the small drawer. I had a plate with a floral design on it and, since the flowers were bold and well-defined, I decided to use the design, omitting the black areas. Since the bright blue colour of the table was so strong, the flower design also needed to be quite pronounced and solid. Decorative detailing such as this could be approached in a number of different ways, such as tracing a design and colouring it, painting freehand, stencilling, or making a *découpage*. For those less used to freehand painting, it is possible to draw the design lightly first, if you use quite a soft pencil such as a 2B. Heavy pencil marks can prove impossible to remove, but soft marks can be wiped off later when the painting is dry.

If you are decorating a drawer, never try to paint it while it is still housed in a cupboard or table. If necessary, sand the edges so that it can be pulled in and out with ease, or alternatively, rub a candle over the edges until the drawer moves freely. Also remember to remove knobs or handles before you begin to paint.

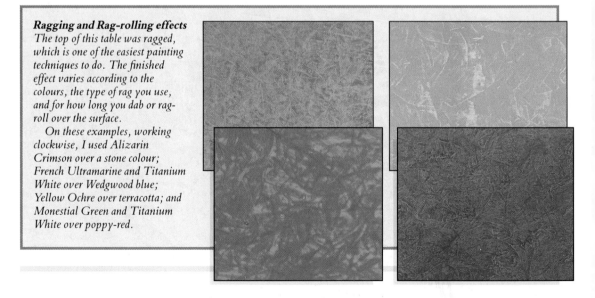

**Ragging and Rag-rolling effects**
*The top of this table was ragged, which is one of the easiest painting techniques to do. The finished effect varies according to the colours, the type of rag you use, and for how long you dab or rag-roll over the surface.*
*On these examples, working clockwise, I used Alizarin Crimson over a stone colour; French Ultramarine and Titanium White over Wedgwood blue; Yellow Ochre over terracotta; and Monestial Green and Titanium White over poppy-red.*

**White spirit**

**Clear glaze** to add to the white spirit and oil colour

**Household brush** for dragging the legs

**Cotton rag** for ragging all over the table top

**Bright blue eggshell** mixed with off-white eggshell for the basecoat

**Clear mid-sheen polyurethane varnish** to seal and protect the surface

**Floral plate** for inspiration, with French Ultramarine, Yellow Ochre, Alizarin Crimson and Permanent Light Green oil colour

**Swordliner** to use with Raw Umber, French Ultramarine and Titanium White oil colour

**Artists' brushes and pencil** for drawing and painting the drawer motif

## METHOD

♦ Paint the piece of furniture with your chosen basecoat and leave it to dry.

♦ For ragging and dragging, make a tinted glaze mixture, keeping the glaze close in tone to the basecoat. For a blue glaze, you must add white eggshell (up to one-third of the total amount) to prevent the glaze from yellowing when dry. Paint the glaze on thinly, and while it is still wet, rag it with a cotton rag or drag it using a household brush.

♦ Find a suitably decorated plate, vase or bowl to use for inspiration, or trace a design of the correct size from a book. Centre the image on the surface of your piece and lightly draw the design with a soft pencil.

♦ Fill in the design with oil colour or acrylic paint. Oil colour is more flexible because it remains workable for some time, but if you are not used to it, use acrylic paint.

♦ For the lining, use oil colour of a darker tone than the basecoat; acrylic paint dries quickly, whereas oil colour can be wiped off if you make mistakes.

♦ Once the surface is dry, apply clear mid-sheen polyurethane varnish to protect the surface. This is particularly important if you use acrylic paint, which chips off quite easily if it is not sealed with varnish.

When I bought this table, the varnish was in good condition, so I keyed the surface with coarse wire wool in order that the paint could adhere to it. I used bright blue eggshell for the basecoat, to which I added a little white eggshell because the blue was too intense. Next, I mixed a tinted glaze of French Ultramarine, Raw Umber and Titanium White oil colour and ragged it over the basecoat. For the legs, I applied the blue glaze with a household brush, then wiped as much glaze as possible off the brush with a rag, and dragged the brush down the legs with sufficient pressure to produce a slightly grainy look.

When painting the freehand flower design, I began by finding the centre of the design's middle flower, then made a paint spot in the centre of the drawer. Next, I added two more spots at a distance of about 2 inches from the knobs to show the limitations of the design, and applied further spots of paint to mark where the other flowers would be placed. I then worked systematically through each colour, filling in the flower shapes with an artist's brush loaded with oil colour.

Finally, using a swordliner and a darker mixture of French Ultramarine, Raw Umber and Titanium White oil colour, I lined the table top.

◀ *The hand-painted flowers add a colourful detail and give the table a focal point. I chose bright tones of green, yellow and blue to match the intensity of the blue ragging.*

▲ *By dragging the legs, I was able to exaggerate the height of the table, adding to its elegance. The dragging also contrasts well with the ragging.*

◀ *I particularly like the way that the table appears to be plain blue from a distance, while up close, you can see the lovely shapes made by the ragging. Lining around the edges in a darker tone frames the table top.*

# WOODGRAINED TRUNK

THIS TRUNK WAS SO suggestive of sunken treasure and swashbuckling pirates that I decided to give it an antique look. Originally, it was quite a rough old chest, with imitation leather along the edges, wooden struts across the top, and rusty metal locks. I could see that it had potential, and I felt sure that all it needed was a simple woodgrained effect, with a little highlighting in places to add interest and a bit of sparkle.

I have been intrigued by the age-old tradition of woodgraining for a long time. At the height of its vogue, every sort of container imaginable was woodgrained, even metal buckets and tin trunks. The art of woodgraining developed to such a degree that one could choose from almost any type of imitation wood, including ash, oak, walnut, rosewood, pine and birdseye maple. Interestingly enough, two Victorian gentlemen, Thomas Kershaw and John Taylor, were so skilled in the art that when they exhibited their woodgrained panels, their handiwork looked so utterly convincing that people refused to believe that the panels were imitation wood without being given proof.

If you wish to do a similar woodgrain finish on a trunk, chest or cupboard, remove any knobs or handles before you begin, and always mask off metal hinges with masking tape before you paint the woodwork. For a woodgrained finish, two browns have to be used; one slightly darker than the other. The paler one is used as a basecoat, with the darker one on top. Using a flogging brush and a comb produces a good effect, but a similar effect can be achieved with an old coarse household brush pushed hard along the surface. The special tool known as a heartgrainer is also fun for woodgraining, once you have mastered the technique of using it.

To paint my trunk, I used a dark tinted glaze of Burnt Umber with a little Alizarin Crimson, over a warm chocolate colour to produce the rich mahogany look. The wax silver cream that I added to the raised nails gives it a little lift – and an added sparkle – in keeping with my theme.

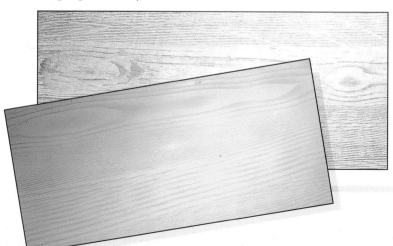

**Woodgraining, and the tools to use**
*With special woodgraining tools, you can create lovely mock wood finishes. Tools include rubber and steel combs; available in various shapes and sizes. Plastic and rubber heartgrainers can also be used to great effect (plastic ones are more durable). For these oak finishes, I used a plastic heartgrainer, a flogging brush, and triangular, and graduated combs.*

**Clear glaze,** to which oil colour and white spirit is added for the tinted glaze mixture

**Household brush** for applying the basecoat

**Poppy – red eggshell and a deep green eggshell basecoat** (mixed together with a small brush)

**White spirit** for the tinted glaze mixture

**Burnt Umber and Alizarin Crimson oil colour** for the tinted glaze

**Flogging brush** to use for the dragging

**Heartgrainer,** to make the "heart" of the wood grain

**Rub-on wax silver cream** with an artist's brush, for highlighting the nails

**Black metal paint** for the metalwork

**Clear mid-sheen polyurethane varnish** to seal the surface and give it a sheen

**Rubber comb** for the woodgraining

## METHOD

♦ First apply your chosen basecoat, and allow it to dry.

♦ Prepare a tinted glaze in a darker tone than that of the basecoat, and paint it thinly all over, concentrating on one side at a time.

♦ Drag and comb the surface while the glaze is wet, to give your piece of furniture a simple woodgrained look. Using different-sized combs together produces a wider variety of woodgrained effects. If you wish, use a heartgrainer on certain areas, pulling it across the surface with a rocking motion. This technique may require a little practice.

♦ When the surface has dried, paint any metal parts with metal paint of a suitable colour. If you wish, rub on a little wax silver cream to add highlights to any raised nails or hinges.

♦ To protect the surface and to give it a slight sheen, apply several coats of clear mid-sheen polyurethane varnish.

▲ The metalwork was painted with black metal paint, which is available in many tones. I then highlighted the raised nails with wax silver cream, which is similar to rub-on wax gilt cream.

◄ The subtle grainy look was produced using a heartgrainer. As its name suggests, the effect looks like the heart of the woodgrain. It takes practice to use one, so experiment first.

I had to rub down all the old metal and remove the rust before I could begin to do any painting. Then I coated the mock leather and wooden struts with a warm brown basecoat (poppy-red eggshell mixed with a deep green). When this was dry, I mixed a tinted glaze, using Burnt Umber and a small amount of Alizarin Crimson oil colour, then applied it thinly all over, and pulled the heartgrainer over some areas to produce a woodgrained look.

The heartgrainer is a simple tool to use, but it takes a little time to use it to perfection. The idea is to pull it across some areas only, using a rocking motion. The rest of the woodgraining can be done with a comb or a flogging brush, depending on whether you want a wide- or close-grained finish.

The metal parts of the trunk were painted with a small brush and some black metal paint, once the rest of the paintwork was dry. To accentuate the metalwork, I painted the rounded nails with some wax silver cream, using a small bristle brush.

# SIMPLE PAINTED FRAMES

PLAIN, SIMPLE MIRROR AND picture frames can be made to look quite exciting if they are painted in bright colours and interesting patterns. On the following five pages, I have decorated frames that are plain and simple in shape, in order to show off the different effects. Most of the other painting techniques in this book can be used successfully to decorate a frame too, but I chose five slightly unusual techniques that are quick, easy, and, with the exception of the gilded frame shown opposite, all experimental.

Some of the frames are more suitable for mirrors, while others are best for pictures. The simple gilt and gesso frame is suitable for either a mirror or a painting, whereas the finger-printed frame might look best on a mirror, and the green dragged frame on a landscape painting. While a frame on a mirror needs to be interesting to liven up the plain glass, a frame on a picture should not distract your eye.

All the frames are made of new wood, so they had to be coated with wood primer first, to seal them. The wood primer soaks into the wood, allowing subsequent coats of paint to lie on the surface rather than soak in. Most wood, especially pine, secretes resin, an orange-coloured sticky substance, which seeps through the layers of paint if you have not sealed the wood first.

You may find that you need to apply more than one basecoat layer, as I did on the frames, sanding between each coat with wet and dry sandpaper for a smooth surface. If you wish to decorate an old frame which is already painted, always remove the existing varnish or peeled paint first, sand the surface, and apply wood primer – it is then ready for the basecoat and your chosen decorative finish.

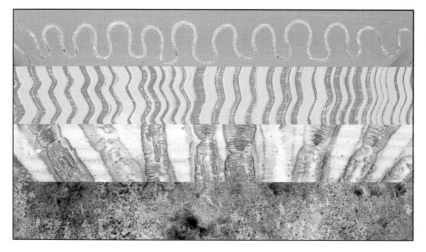

*On each of the painted frames on the following pages, I used colours that I particularly like. You could use whatever colour scheme you prefer, as long as the basecoat and tinted glaze complement each other well. This is especially important if you are doing a technique in which the basecoat shows through, for example, where you have combed, dragged or scratched the surface, as illustrated by these details.*

## GILT AND GESSO FRAME

*To decorate this frame, I used ready-made gesso and rub-on wax gilt cream. The pot of gesso needs to stand in a pan of hot water until it has melted, and can then be applied with a brush. When the surface was dry, I rubbed on the gilt cream sparingly with my finger, so that the red gesso would show through in some places.*

## SQUIGGLE-SCRATCHED FRAME

*For this frame, I used Raw Sienna and Titanium White acrylic paint. Next, I added Cobalt Blue to the mixture to produce an unusual greeny-grey. Then, with an old household brush, I dragged each side of the frame. I allowed it to dry, then using the wooden end of my brush, I drew a squiggly line all around the frame, removing the top colour to reveal the base.*

## ZIG-ZAG COMBED FRAME

*On this frame, I used a favourite old rubber comb made specifically for woodgraining. I applied two coats of poppy-red eggshell for the basecoat, to show through wherever I combed. When this was dry, I mixed Oxide of Chromium with a little Titanium White acrylic, painted the frame one side at a time, then combed it quickly, and moved on to comb the next side.*

## FINGER-PRINTED FRAME

*This frame reminds me of tie-dye fabric. I began with black eggshell, followed by a combination of white and yellow. I coated my brush with a thin wash of white acrylic, dipped the corner into the yellow paint, and painted the frame, keeping the yellow side of the brush at the outside. Then, pressing my finger flat on the surface, pointing inwards, I finger-printed around the frame.*

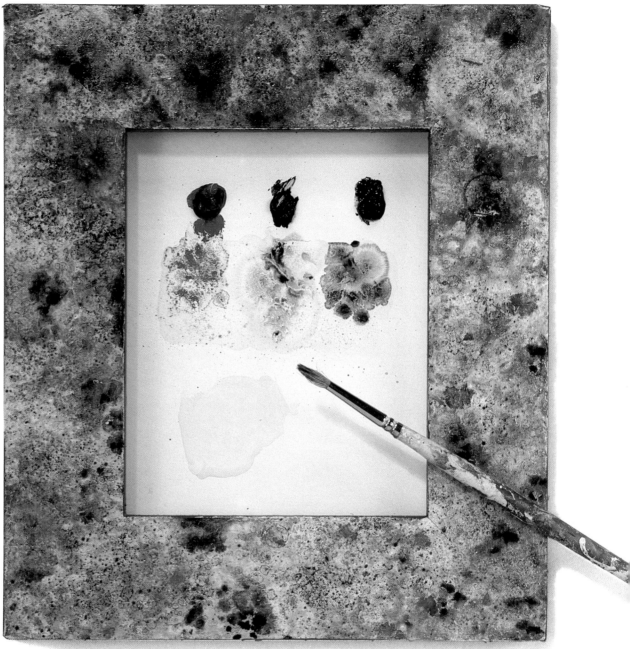

## MOTTLED SPATTER FRAME

*I coated this frame with off-white eggshell, then applied some polyurethane varnish. While the varnish was wet, I dropped a mixture of Burnt Umber, Monestial Green and Alizarin Crimson oil colour on to it, by touching different areas with the tip of a brush. I also spattered the frame by tapping the loaded brush with my finger, flicking dots of paint over certain areas with my thumb.*

# DÉCOUPAGE CABINET

THIS CABINET was quite a bargain, and it was easy to decide on the sort of look I wanted for its decoration. Soon I had quite a firm idea about how I would paint it, and for this reason, I chose emulsion and acrylic paint, both of which are quick-drying.

I believe the cabinet had been designed as a bedside table, and it was basically made of plywood with a thin, dull, ugly veneer over it, which had peeled off in parts, leaving it looking very shabby. The owner of the junk shop where I found the cabinet was only too pleased to get rid of it. In spite of its dull surface appearance, I was attracted by its somewhat classical shape, and could imagine how different it would look if painted in another colour. As it was essentially quite elegant in shape, with its curving legs, I felt it should have an eighteenth-century look. I found my inspiration when I came across a picture of an Italian commode, incorporating cut-outs.

I had already decided that at some time I would do a *découpage*, which I had always thought of as Victorian in origin. After reading and browsing over various furniture books, I discovered that Italians in the eighteenth century had used the technique to help mass produce large quantities of highly-decorated furniture. *L'arte del povero* ("poor man's art") arose when apprentice artists, in order to meet the demand for ornate furniture, began to colour prints and engravings of the old masters, and glue them to the surfaces of desks and jewel boxes, to which they added several coats of lacquer. This European process was an inexpensive way of imitating Oriental lacquerwork. The Victorians soon adopted the art of *découpage*, and made it a popular household craft by using cards and pictures to decorate chimney boards, screens and boxes.

**Choosing découpage images**
*Almost any picture from a magazine or a greetings card is suitable for a découpage, as long as no pictures or printed type on the reverse side show through. Alternatively, you can buy paper cut-outs which are expressly designed to use for a découpage.*

*These two examples are taken from a book of découpage images that I often use. Once you have cut out the pictures, colour them with water-based paint or crayons. I used conté crayons to lightly colour in the unicorn, and my childrens' wax crayons for the knave.*

**Wet and dry sandpaper** *to soften the whole effect*

**Off-white emulsion,** *to be mixed with Raw Umber and Permanent Yellow acrylic paint for the basecoat, with a household brush*

**Book of** découpage **images** *to use for inspiration, with spray adhesive for sticking on the cut-outs*

**Masking tape** *for the lining*

**Sharp scalpel**

**Small artist's brush**

**Raw Umber and Emerald Green acrylic paint** *for the lining*

**Clear mid-sheen polyurethane varnish**

**Yellow Ochre, Prussian Blue and Alizarin Crimson gouache** *for painting the* découpage

## METHOD

♦ Paint the item with the basecoat of your choice and allow it to dry completely.

♦ Next, apply several tones of your chosen water-based paint, to make a subtle variation of colour all over.

♦ Once this is dry, line around the edges in a complementary colour, laying down two strips of masking tape first to keep your lining straight. If using acrylic paint, apply it without water, or with very little, since it dries quickly.

♦ Cut out your scraps with a sharp craft knife, then test their positions, using masking tape. If you wish, colour them and let them dry.

♦ When they are dry, apply a small amount of glue or spray adhesive to the scraps, and stick them firmly in position. Squeeze any excess glue out to the edges, as this will affect the flatness of the cut-outs.

♦ Apply clear mid-sheen polyurethane varnish four times, allowing at least six hours' drying time between coats. Apply the varnish thinly in the direction of the wood grain, for a dragged effect. In the final coat, add a little oil colour to "dirty" it. Leave it to dry.

♦ Using wet and dry sandpaper, rub some areas back to the basecoat. Rub over the cut-outs to break up the edges, then reapply the tinted varnish. Sand again if you wish, then varnish the surface one more time.

First I had to glue down the loose veneer on the cabinet. Then I stripped it and rubbed it down with coarse wire wool and a cloth soaked in white spirit. In removing the veneer around the edges, I was left with a rough surface, and decided that the overall look of the piece would have to be distressed because it had such an uneven finish. Removing the veneer in parts was also helpful in recreating an elegant Italian piece dating back to the eighteenth century, that was distressed and ravaged with time.

To achieve an interesting worn look, I painted on a mixture of off-white emulsion with Raw Umber and Permanent Yellow acrylic paint, keeping the tones close. This was left to dry. Masking tape was laid down, leaving an edge, and these borders were painted in a mixture of Emerald Green and Raw Umber acrylic so that some parts were deep emerald and others were more muted. I removed the masking tape quickly so that it would not adhere to the paint too much and peel it off.

From a widely-available book of *découpage* designs, I decided on cherubs after rejecting baskets of fruit, which were not really strong enough images for the design of this piece. The original knobs on the doors were made of unattractive brown plastic, so I replaced them with elegant brass knobs. A key hanging from a tassel would suit this piece too.

▲ *I added a hand-painted line to the top of the legs, to echo and highlight their curved shape.*

▶ *Once I had coloured the cherubs with gouache paint, and allowed them to dry completely, I stuck them down with spray adhesive, applied very thinly.*

◀ *When lining, lay down the masking tape lightly to use as a guide. When the painted line has dried, lift the tape off briskly.*

# HAND-PAINTED CUPBOARD

 A SMALL HANGING CUPBOARD such as this has many uses, for example, in a child's room, a workroom, bathroom or kitchen. While the cupboard did not look very promising at first glance, I remembered something that I had seen in *The World of Interiors* magazine which had impressed me with its vibrant decoration. It was a piece by the French artist and furniture-maker, Gérard Rigot, who specializes in furniture with an emphasis on rustic simplicity and primary colours. I really liked his hanging cupboard made from an old window frame, with its brightly-painted panels and simple fruit-tree motifs.

I experimented with different proportions of my chosen colours, rubbing them on and off the cupboard in areas of interest, and working them into the corners and mouldings. The two little framed panelled doors seemed to invite the addition of pictures but, since the cupboard was not beautifully finished off, I felt that the pictures should be quite naive in style. I thought that here, too, trees would suit the piece well. One final touch was to add some free-spirited dabs of paint to emphasize the overall rustic feeling. In the end, with only a few colours and brushes, I was able to make my hanging cupboard look quite decorative, and unusual too.

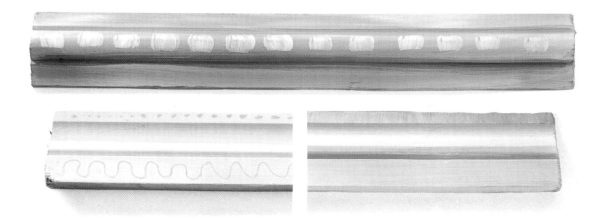

**Freehand painted effects**
*These three examples may give you some ideas on how to decorate the carved areas on your furniture. The joy of freehand painting is that you do not need to be a competent artist to produce effective results.*

*Simple freehand dots and dashes can look very pretty, as on the hanging cupboard. On the examples above, I dabbed a flat-ended brush over the grey moulding, then used the pointed handle to "scratch" a squiggly line along the yellow moulding.*

*With the tip of an artist's brush, I added bright yellow dots along the edge of the yellow moulding. On the pink one, I highlighted certain areas with a darker tone, brushing it along the inner edge with a small brush in an irregular way, to add interest.*

**Pale primrose-coloured emulsion** *for the basecoat*

**Hoghair fitch brush** *for painting in the corners*

**Household brush** *for applying the basecoat and the varnish*

**Clear mid-sheen polyurethane varnish** *to give a hard-wearing protective finish*

**Burnt Sienna, Raw Umber and Oxide of Chromium acrylic paint** *mixed with pale primrose emulsion in varying amounts for the decorative effects*

**Small soft nylon brush** *and artist's sable brush for dabbing on the colour*

---

## METHOD

♦ First apply your chosen basecoat and allow it to dry.

♦ To add interest, apply a darker tone of your basecoat colour to focal points such as corners and mouldings. This detailing is probably best done with acrylic paints, and a small brush to give you greater control.

♦ To highlight these details, rub a lighter tone on top, allowing some dark areas to show through. You need very little paint on the brush for this, and you have to rub, rather than brush to achieve the right effect.

♦ For extra decorative detailing, take a small, soft nylon or artist's brush, and dab colour on in spots and dashes wherever you wish, using colours which complement the basecoat colour. Make the spot with the tip, and the dash with the length of the brush.

♦ When your paintwork is dry, protect the surface with a coat of clear mid-sheen polyurethane varnish.

To colour the ridged mouldings and corners, I applied a mixture of Burnt Sienna acrylic paint and a pale primrose-coloured emulsion with a hoghair fitch. To soften the lines and give it a painterly look, I rubbed colour on to the cupboard with the side of my brush. Burnt Sienna, Oxide of Chromium acrylic paint and pale primrose emulsion were applied to the semi-circular corner pieces. To frame my tree motifs, I coated the brush unevenly with Raw Umber and pale primrose, dragging the brush down either side of the panels. When this was dry, I added dots and dashes around the edges and a circlet of leaves and berries around the hanging holes, then sealed the paintwork with clear mid-sheen polyurethane varnish.

# HAND-PAINTED CHEST

I BOUGHT THIS OAK chest of drawers because I was attracted by its simple, solid shape and copper handles. It was not a classic Georgian or Victorian piece, which I would normally drag and line in a traditional way, but a modern design, so I felt the need to age it a little, to make it look more interesting. I decided on an unusual experimental approach, bleaching it first, then hand-painting it in a naive way with masking fluid. This treatment not only works well on furniture for a child's bedroom, where the images could tone in with all the toys and games around, but also in a rustic-style kitchen or dining-room, blending in with other old pieces of furniture.

The combination of oak and copper was favoured by furniture-makers of the Arts and Crafts Movement, but judging by the lack of adornment and the general shape, I think this chest was most likely to have been factory-made. Its slightly rough feel was reminiscent of the off-beat designs of the Bloomsbury Set that I have seen, where a single motif is used in a free, painterly way. I began to think about using a single motif for the top of the chest something simple yet immediately recognizable, which would suit the shape. Since the surface was long and thin, it was not easy to find an appropriate single motif. After looking through some of my books, I decided on the image of a lion with a swishing tail. I then added a series of plain squares down the front, also inspired by the Arts and Crafts style, which completed the design without detracting from the more decorative treatment of the lion on the top.

**Using masking fluid in freehand painting**
*The lion design on the chest was painted with the help of some masking fluid. You can paint quite freely with masking fluid and a brush, to make all sorts of interesting patterns.*

*Here is an example of the stages involved in the process; applying the masking fluid, painting over the hardened fluid, and peeling it off later to reveal areas of bare wood.*

**White spirit** *for the tinted glaze mixture*

**Wood bleach** *to lighten the wood before hand-painting it*

**Clear mid-sheen poly-urethane varnish** *mixed in a jam jar with white spirit, and tinted with Viridian Green, then prepared again, using French Ultra-marine oil colour*

**Household brush** *for applying the wood bleach*

**Viridian Green and French Ultramarine oil colour** *for the two tinted glaze mixtures*

**Masking fluid,** *to be applied with a bristle brush*

**Cerulean Blue and Raw Umber acrylic paint** *to use with an eraser for printing the rectangles*

**Flat-ended nylon brush** *for filling in the rectangular shapes with colour*

**Images from a book of** découpage **designs** – *the inspiration for the lion on the top of the chest*

**Beeswax polish** *to use with a mutton cloth to buff the painted surface*

---

## METHOD

♦ Lightly draw your image in pencil, then paint those areas you wish to "reverse out" with masking fluid. If you make a mistake, let the masking fluid dry, peel it off and start again.

♦ Once the masking fluid has dried, fill in the design with a thin mixture of clear polyurethane varnish and white spirit, tinted with different colours as appropriate.

♦ When these areas are dry, peel off the masking fluid, revealing the light wood underneath. If the surface looks too dark, rub it back with fine wire wool, or apply a thinned coat of light-coloured eggshell and wipe it off quickly.

♦ To add rectangular or square shapes, print with an old eraser and acrylic paint, then fill in the shapes with a flat-ended brush loaded with more paint.

♦ If you wish to age the piece, apply a thinned coat of light-coloured eggshell when the surface is dry, and wipe it off quickly.

♦ Alternatively, to preserve the newness of your paint-work, polish the surface with some beeswax on a soft cloth.

Decorating this chest was a challenge. Before painting, I removed all the old varnish, hoping to find a lighter wood underneath, but it was still too dark. After bleaching the front five times, the wood was finally light enough.

For the design, I used masking fluid, drawing the shape of a lion in freehand. When the masking fluid had dried, I half-filled a jam jar with clear polyurethane varnish, white spirit and a little Viridian Green oil colour, and painted it on, then made a similar mixture using French Ultramarine for the sky. When my paintwork was dry, I peeled off the masking fluid to reveal the light wood underneath. The painted areas looked a little dark compared to the light wood, so I rubbed them back with fine wire wool. Then, with thinned white eggshell, I painted the whole surface to lighten and age it.

The front needed a detail to give it a lift, and small rectangles placed regularly down each side solved the problem. I used a ruler to mark roughly where the centre of each square should be, and lightly printed with an old eraser, filling in the shapes afterwards with a flat-ended brush and some more paint.

*When drawing with masking fluid and a brush, remember that wherever you "paint" with the fluid, the surface will actually be unpainted when you have finished. It is best to experiment with masking fluid and some colour on a spare piece of wood before using it on your furniture. For my lion design, I finally chose a combination of Viridian Green and French Ultramarine.*

# MARBLED TABLE

AFTER SEARCHING OVER SEVERAL months for a suitable table to use in my hallway, I finally found this one in an old junk shop. Although the pine legs were well-shaped, and the drawer looked interesting with its slight outward curve, the table top itself was completely useless, part of it having broken off completely. Judging by the deep saw marks in the wood, I imagine it had spent most of its life as a carpenter's work-bench. Before I could begin to do any painting, a new table top had to be made, since the existing one was beyond repair. As I intended to do a *faux marbre* effect, there was no point in having a new pine table top made, so I used MDF (medium density fibreboard), which is an excellent surface to work on, as it takes paint extremely well.

In designing my own *faux marbre* finish, I was able to choose colours that comple-mented the colour scheme of my home perfectly. I chose Raw Umber and off-white as the main colours, with Burnt Sienna and Light Red to add a little warmth. These were similar tones to the colourwashed walls of the hall where my table was to stand. In choosing colours for marbling, it is best to keep to cold greys, misty blues, muddy yellows and earthy greens, because they will look more realistic than bright tones such as emerald green or brilliant yellow. Although bold colours do occur in real marble, the novice is wise to work in subtle tones.

I spent a long time looking at marble furniture before embarking on the technique, since it was important to make myself familiar with the characteristics of real marble. It is a good idea to take the time to do this, as it gives you a useful understanding of the patterns and shapes, and may help to make your *faux marbre* look more convincing.

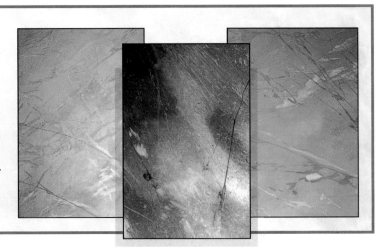

### Creating the look of marble

*Marbling, with a tinted glaze of the appropriate colour, can look incredibly realistic, as shown by these examples. For the bright yellow marbling, I used a tinted glaze of Raw Sienna, Titanium White and a little Raw Umber. I added more Titanium White for the pale yellow marble. The smokey-grey marbling was done using Raw Umber, Prussian Blue and Titanium White. Then, to create pale areas, I wiped on Titanium White.*

**Off-white eggshell** *for the basecoat and marbling*

**Clear glaze**

**Cotton rag** *for removing colour at the veining stage*

**Raw Umber oil colour** *for the tinted glaze mixture, and for lining the legs of the table*

**White spirit** *for the tinted glaze mixture*

**Softening brush** *to blend the tones together a little*

**Burnt Umber and Light Red oil colour** *for the tinted glaze mixture*

**Small bristle brush** *for the marbling*

**Small flat nylon brush** *for painting the panel shapes*

**Clear, mid-sheen polyurethane varnish** *to protect the table top and produce a marble-like sheen*

**Household brush** *for the varnish*

**Mutton cloth** *to dab over the surface to remove the brush marks*

## METHOD

◆ Apply your basecoat and allow it to dry. You may need several coats for a smooth foundation on which to marble. Sand the final coat with wet and dry sandpaper.

◆ Prepare a tinted glaze, using slightly more white spirit than clear glaze, and add oil colour to suit.

◆ Begin to marble the top, using the tinted glaze and a bristle brush or a hoghair fitch, working in a diagonal direction. Wipe off some areas with a dry brush where the lighter areas are to be, or dab on a little white oil colour.

◆ With a mutton cloth, dab the surface to remove the brush marks, then use a softening brush to blend the colours. This technique requires practice, but it will transform your patchy colours into smooth-looking marble.

◆ If necessary to your design, add distressing and veining, and do the veining diagonally, as it is on real marble. Finally, to balance with the marbled top, drag or rag the legs of your piece.

◆ Leave the marbling to dry, preferably overnight. Apply two coats of clear, non-yellowing, mid-sheen polyurethane varnish to protect the surface and to produce the characteristic sheen of real marble.

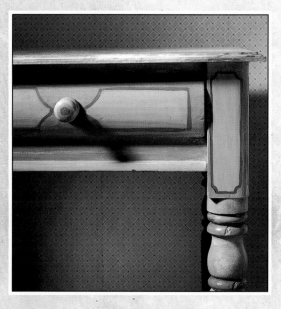

First of all, I painted the table in off-white egg-shell, which emphasized the deep cracks in the legs and revealed dozens of woodworm holes. When the surface was dry, I treated the wood-worm, but left the cracks because they added character to the piece. Then I applied two more coats of eggshell to the top, and rubbed down the final coat with wet and dry sandpaper. Next, I mixed a tinted glaze, using off-white eggshell, Raw Umber, Burnt Sienna and Light Red oil colour, which makes a good all-purpose tone that works well in many places.

When I came to paint the legs, I tried drag-ging them in the same colours as the marbling, adding greens and blue-greys, but nothing looked right. I realized that they needed greater detailing to balance with the marble top, so I lined them in Raw Umber, with little black and white panel shapes to add definition. I made similar shapes on the drawer and side panels, then added lines to the legs, which completed the look. Finally, to bring the marbled finish alive, I varnished the top with clear, mid-sheen polyurethane varnish three times and the legs and drawer twice.

# Hand-Painted Chairs

One of my first introductions to painted furniture was through Pennsylvania Dutch work – the folk art style which was promoted in the latter part of the eighteenth century by German settlers in Pennsylvania, who decorated all kinds of furniture and domestic items. Favourite motifs were flowers and birds, and many of the images chosen had symbolic connotations. One of their charming traditions was to date and initial their furniture, sometimes adding uplifting Biblical quotations.

Modern versions of this folk art style are being made by Moyra Bannister, a lady of Swedish origin who has painted many pieces for her children incorporating their names, with appropriate phrases for birthdays, weddings and christenings. Her work prompted me to decorate the green and yellow chair in a similar manner, which I did for my mother, who I knew would appreciate this style of paintwork.

The black chair's decoration was influenced by something completely different – namely, all the beautiful black *papier mâché* items that I have seen, usually trays, screens and table tops. The art of *papier mâché* originated in the Far East; by the eighteenth century it had spread to France, and by the nineteenth century to the rest of Europe. In the mid-nineteenth century, when sophisticated manufacturing methods were invented, the industry was at its height. The items produced at that time usually incorporated landscapes and flower designs, the most extravagant of which were inlaid with mother-of-pearl, and had gilt edgings. In addition to flowers, birds and butterflies often appeared on black backgrounds, hand-painted to give a deep luxurious patina. On my hand-painted *papier mâché*-inspired chair, I have incorporated a modern imitation of mother-of-pearl that might have astonished the Victorians.

**Alternative ideas for painted effects**
*Hand-painting your furniture can be great fun, but for those with little confidence in their artistic ability, here are some easy alternatives. Squiggle-scratching, combing, printing and distressing – all these finishes look effective and pretty.*

**Eggshell varnish,** to seal and protect the painted chairs

**Household brush**

**Black eggshell basecoat** for the black chair

**Green eggshell basecoat** for the green chair

**Crimson, Permanent Yellow, Cerulean Blue, Emerald, Titanium White and Yellow Ochre acrylic paint** for the green chair

**Titanium White, Alizarin Crimson, Raw Umber, Oxide of Chromium, Yellow Ochre, Prussian Blue and Indian Red oil colour** for the black chair

**Three small artists' brushes** for painting the designs on the chairs

**Rub-on wax gilt cream and nail polish** for the black chair

## METHOD

### FOR BOTH CHAIRS

◆ Apply your chosen basecoat and allow it to dry (mid-sheen eggshell paint is an ideal choice).

◆ Decide on your design, and experiment on paper before you begin to paint.

◆ Draw the design lightly on your chair with a soft pencil, or, if you prefer, use a stencil.

◆ Using acrylic paint, which dries more quickly than oil colour, paint over your drawn design in freehand, or apply the colour through a stencil, if you prefer.

◆ To add the mother-of-pearl effect as shown on the *papier mâché*-style chair, apply two or three coats of pearlized nail polish to certain areas. When the nail polish is dry, wipe a little pure oil colour over some parts, to add a hint of pinky-mauve.

◆ For the *papier mâché*-style chair only, add a little gilt cream to certain carved areas, when all the paintwork is completely dry.

◆ Finish off your handiwork by applying one or two coats of clear mid-sheen polyurethane varnish, to seal and protect the painted surface.

## FOLK ART-STYLE CHAIR

I decided to paint a folk art-style chair for my mother because she loves bright colours, and always likes to have pieces of furniture that I have painted, so it was a particular pleasure to decorate this piece especially for her.

I painted the two birds in freehand, with the date and my mother's initials, D.S., on the top. Someone without confidence in their drawing ability could produce the same effect, by using a traditional Pennsylvania Dutch design from a book of stencils.

## PAPIER MÂCHÉ-STYLE CHAIR

The decoration of the *papier mâché*-style chair, I thought of as something of a trick, since the imitation mother-of-pearl flowers were to be made from pearlized nail polish, highlighted with a little oil colour.

I drew my floral arrangement on paper first, then outlined the design on the chair in pencil and selected which petals were to be pearlized. Once I had applied sufficient nail polish and allowed it to dry, I added a hint of mauve by wiping pure oil colour over some areas.

# COMBED CHEST OF DRAWERS

THIS CHEST OF DRAWERS is a solid piece of furniture with plenty of storage space, and similar old chests are widely available. When I discovered this one in our local junk shop, I wondered if it might be appropriate for my childrens' bedroom, decorated in a suitable colour to tone in with the pale blue walls. Chests like this are sturdy enough to last a lifetime, and a different decorative finish at every stage, from infancy to adulthood, ensures that they will not be discarded.

Among the decorative finishes that would have worked well on this piece are stippling, spattering, ragging and combing. I finally chose to do the latter because it produced a robust finish suitable for young children, and because the chest had been combed originally. The earlier finish was a combed woodgrained effect, but the chest was damaged to such an extent when I bought it that a large piece had splintered off one of the drawers, leaving a deep scar in the wood.

The technique of combing is thought to have originated in Ancient Egypt, where leather and wooden combs were used in decorative paintwork to simulate real wood grain. Combing has also been a popular technique in European folk art for centuries, and also with early Scandinavian and German settlers in America.

At the moment, my combed chest of drawers stands on the landing, having proved invaluable for storing towels and linen. I imagine that by the time the boys need it in their room, I may even have decorated it again in a totally different way!

***Creating your own combed patterns***
*A variety of exciting effects can be produced using combs of different shapes and sizes (see Combing, p.108). For these examples, I used two graduated combs, and one plastic triangular comb, which has differently-spaced teeth on each side.*

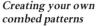

**Tinted glaze mixture**

**Off-white eggshell** basecoat

**Clear glaze** to mix with oil colour and white spirit for the tinted glaze

**Mutton cloths** for wiping the excess glaze off the combs

**White spirit** for the tinted glaze mixture

**Household brush** to use with the eggshell basecoat

**Hoghair fitch** for applying the tinted glaze

**Flat bristle brush** and artist's brush for the details

**Cobalt Blue, Monestial Green and Burnt Umber oil colour** for the tinted glaze mixture

**Combs** of two different types, to give a variety of effects

Before I began the surface decoration, the chest needed a fair amount of wood filler to repair the scratches. All the knobs had to be replaced, as I was unable to match the missing ones because they were so unusual.

I decided to comb the chest only after my attempts at dragging proved unsatisfactory. First, I applied three coats of off-white eggshell, sanding each layer in between for a smooth surface, then dragged the chest in yellow. The overall effect was too pale, so I tried dragging in green, but it still did not produce the effect that I wanted. The marvellous thing about tinted glazes is that they are so versatile. Mistakes can either be wiped off while the surface is wet, or allowed to dry, with a different colour applied on top. Although the green and yellow paintwork was eventually covered up, both colours show through just enough to enhance, and give substance to the blue combing.

In the end, I chose combing because it is a tough finish which would look effective over all the previous paint layers. I chose a mixture of green and blue to match the walls in the boys' room, adding a little Burnt Umber to deepen the tone.

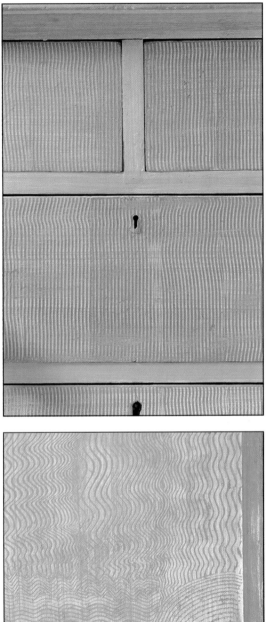

▼ *Always remove any handles or knobs before you begin to decorate your piece, and only replace them once the paintwork is dry. For added interest, decorate the knobs with a colour and design to match your piece.*

▶ *The lightly dragged framework around the drawer-fronts adds definition and also contrasts well with the combing. On the top, I combed a crazy, wavy pattern, which gives a lift to the large, plain surface.*

# MUTTON-CLOTHED BEDSTEAD

WHEN I ACQUIRED THIS lovely bed, the wood was stained a deep orange-red, which was far too strong a colour for such a heavy piece of furniture. The twisted barley-sugar bedposts and carved heraldic crests captured my imagination, and I decided to decorate the bed in such a way as to soften its appearance, making it more restful to the eye and thus more conducive to sleep. The finished bed is quite romantic, atmospheric of favourite fairy tales.

A bedstead presents one with much scope for decoration, and many techniques are suitable, including stippling, marbling, woodgraining, stencilling and freehand painting. However, since this piece was already busy with carving and ornate bedposts, it only needed a simple decorative effect, so I chose a technique known as "mutton-clothing".

During the nineteenth century, decorative painted furniture was mainly restricted to the rooms where it could be displayed and shown off to friends, therefore antique painted chairs, tables and cupboards are much easier to find than bedsteads. In some Germanic peasant communities, however, particularly Bavaria, painted bedroom furniture played an important role in a bride's dowry. Bedsteads made of untreated wood were often stencilled on directly, with black outlining added to highlight the stencil. Late eighteenth-century German immigrants in Pennsylvania, the Pennsylvania Dutch, decorated almost all their furniture, painting bedsteads with flower and bird motifs. Our modern-day bedroom furniture looks quite tame in comparison.

***Mutton-clothing as a decorative technique***
*Mutton-clothing is a simple technique, which consists of dabbing over a tinted glaze with a mutton cloth to produce a soft, irregular, cloudy effect. The cloth, also known as stockinet, resembles a dish-cloth, and as you dab, it leaves a pattern of the weave on the surface, absorbing more colour in some areas than others.*

*On these examples, I used an off-white basecoat, and, from left to right, Burnt Umber and French Ultramarine; Indian Red and Titanium White; and Cerulean Blue, Titanium White and Burnt Umber.*

**Off-white eggshell** *for the basecoat*

**White spirit** *to mix with clear glaze and oil colour for the tinted glaze*

**Household brush** *for applying the eggshell basecoat*

**Clear glaze** *for the tinted glaze mixture*

**Mutton cloth** *for dabbing off the colour to produce a soft hazy finish*

**Venetian Red oil colour** *for the tinted glaze mixture*

**Clear mid-sheen polyurethane varnish** *to seal and protect the painted surface*

**Clean cotton rag** *to wipe over the carved areas, to contrast with the mutton-clothing*

## METHOD

♦ Apply a basecoat of your choice, and leave it to dry. For a really smooth surface, you may need to apply more than one basecoat layer, sanding in between with wet and dry sandpaper. This will provide a foundation on which to do the mutton-clothing.

♦ Prepare a tinted glaze, using a little more oil colour than usual, since the mutton cloth will absorb much of the colour.

♦ Apply the tinted glaze, and while it is still wet, dab over it with a mutton cloth. As the cloth becomes covered in glaze, refold it, and use it again. If the piece of furniture is large, you may need to use more than one mutton cloth as the first one becomes too sticky to use.

♦ Once you have finished, go over any raised, carved or moulded areas with a clean cotton rag, wiping off some areas of colour to add a little definition and contrast. If you prefer, highlight these areas with another tone instead.

♦ Once the surface is dry, seal it with clear mid-sheen polyurethane varnish, if you wish.

I began by painting the bedposts and headboard, dabbing over the wet painted surface with a mutton cloth. For large pieces of furniture, you may need to use several mutton cloths, since they soon become sticky as they absorb the tinted glaze.

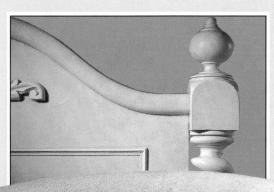

To contrast with the mutton-clothing, I wiped over the carved motif with a clean cotton rag, to lighten the heraldic shape. As an alternative, the carved areas could be painted in a complementary tone, or highlighted with some wax gilt cream.

I thought the colour scheme for the bed ought to be pale because it was such a large and heavy piece of furniture. I chose a tinted glaze of Venetian Red oil colour, and lightened it a little by adding off-white eggshell. Also, because the bedstead was large, I decided to paint it in sections so that the glaze would remain wet enough for me to dab over it with a cloth.

I began by painting the four bedposts, each of which was dabbed over with a mutton cloth. Next, I decorated the head- and footboards. To give the finish a little more definition, I took a clean cotton rag and wiped it over the carved heraldic device and the rectangular moulding. If there had been no carving, I would have marbled the central panel, or added a stencil.

# SPONGED HANGING CUPBOARD

 THIS PRETTY PINE CUPBOARD was originally a dingy Victorian medicine cupboard, stained a dark mahogany colour, and heavy and dull in appearance. It was in desperate need of brightening up, but I wanted the overall effect to be soft and subtle, to tone in with my bathroom. The large, flat, panelled areas seemed ideal for sponging on, and this technique also seemed particularly appropriate for the bathroom setting. Sponging is one of the easiest and quickest finishes to do, and looks effective on most surfaces, creating a lightly speckled finish. You may find it rewarding to sponge with several different colours too, but it is important to keep them close in tone as I have done here, in order to prevent them from jarring.

To complement the colour scheme of the bathroom, I chose subtle tones of Light Red and Yellow Ochre oil colour mixed with a little off-white eggshell. I sponged the cupboard twice, because initially, the sponging looked too peach-coloured. By adding a little Alizarin Crimson and off-white eggshell to the original tinted glaze, I managed to create the colour that I wanted. To complete the look, I painted each of the edges with a purplish rose colour, which adds definition to the sponging, and also serves to frame the cupboard rather well.

***Producing different effects with a sponge***
*The variety of effects that can be produced with sponging is enormous, as illustrated by these four examples. The end result not only depends on the colours you choose, but on how much pressure you apply to the surface, and for how long you sponge. The effect can be soft and hazy, or patchy and irregular.*

*With these examples, working clockwise, I used Monestial Green, Titanium White and Burnt Umber over pink; Monestial Green over Wedgwood blue; Alizarin Crimson and Titanium White over grey; and Yellow Ochre over grey.*

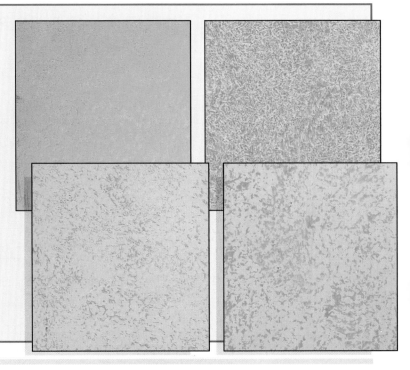

**Pale brown eggshell,** *to mix with Oxide of Chromium oil colour for the mouse-brown basecoat*

**White spirit** *for the tinted glaze mixture*

**Clear glaze** *to mix with white spirit and oil colour for the tinted glaze*

**Household brush** *for the basecoat, and for dragging certain areas*

**Oxide of Chromium** *oil colour*

**Yellow Ochre and Light Red** *oil colour, to mix with off-white eggshell for the sponging*

**Off-white eggshell** *to add to Light Red and Yellow Ochre oil colour for the sponging*

**Small, flat bristle brush,** *with Alizarin Crimson oil colour to mix with a little Oxide of Chromium for the edges*

**Natural sponge** *to dab over the surface, to produce the soft speckled finish*

## METHOD

♦ Apply your basecoat and allow it to dry completely.

♦ For the sponging, prepare a tinted glaze, keeping the colour close in tone to the basecoat. When sponging, it is important to keep the colours close in tone, to give depth, and to achieve a soft, cloudy finish.

♦ Dip a natural sponge lightly into the colour and dab it gently over the surface. Vary the pressure a little, but aim for an even overall pattern. Use more than one tone if you wish, allowing each to dry first, or, alternatively, sponge two or more tones while they are still wet, so that they merge.

♦ If you wish to add some definition to the sponging, drag the raised, carved or moulded areas with a household brush of the appropriate size. Dragging contrasts well with sponging.

♦ When the surface is completely dry, apply a coat of clear, mid-sheen polyurethane varnish to seal and protect the surface.

The dark mahogany varnish on this pine cupboard was several layers thick, so I had to remove it all before I could begin to do the sponging. With some varnish remover and a scraper, I stripped off the old varnish, cleaning the more intricate parts with coarse wire wool soaked in white spirit.

For the basecoat, I bought a pale brown eggshell, but when I began to paint, the colour looked much too pink. To counteract this, I added some Oxide of Chromium oil colour, which produced exactly the mouse-brown colour that I had wanted. For the sponging, I made a warm pink tinted glaze, using Light Red and Yellow Ochre oil colour, with a little off-white eggshell. I mixed the tinted glaze unevenly, so that sometimes the sponge would pick up more Light Red, and at other times, more off-white and Yellow Ochre. I sponged this all over the panelled areas, then dragged the sides with a household brush, adding a little Alizarin Crimson to the original tinted glaze.

Finally, to contrast with the sponged areas, I painted the edges with a purple mixture of Alizarin Crimson and Oxide of Chromium oil colour, using a small, flat-ended brush. This paint took a long time to dry, because I did not add clear glaze to the mixture. I therefore waited a few days before adding a coat of clear midsheen polyurethane varnish.

# LIMED, STENCILLED TABLE

ONE OF THE MOST attractive qualities of this small pine table was its rough, and slightly weatherbeaten wood grain. Originally, it must have been a card-table because the baize top had been removed. The rough wood underneath was exposed and the rest of the table had been varnished and partly stripped, so that some areas were dark and some light. I rather liked this effect, and therefore left the areas of varnish as they were, and simply painted a thin layer of blue-grey over the top and wiped it, allowing the different tones to show through. This effect copies the traditional technique of limewashing, a method used in farming districts many years ago. Lime, which is a caustic substance, was used on furniture and walls to clean the rooms up – literally, too, since lime has disinfectant properties. Real limewash is powdery and does not last long. An identical but lasting effect can be achieved by using either a wax kit or paint. This involves brushing on colour and wiping it off so that crevices and uneven spots in the wood hold the colour, while only a pale covering of paint remains on smoother areas. I wanted to achieve a bleached effect.

My choice of colour was largely influenced by Scandinavian furniture and folk art that I find so interesting. The wreath stencil with berries is a traditional motif found in many cultures. I chose to make a double wreath of two leaves on each side of the berries in order to add bulk to the design. A leaf is one of the easiest shapes to create with a stencil because your hand curves naturally when you are cutting it out. On the legs, and along the edges, I painted some more crudely-cut stencils of arabesques and curlicues for a balanced design. The finished table appears to radiate the warmth of Scandinavian summers combined with the seasonal cheer of Christmas.

### Liming with different colour combinations

*Liming provides the ideal background for a stencil, as they complement each other so well. Before I limed my table, I experimented with several tones of blue, green, and peach. I decided that the table should be light blue, to make the stencil the main feature.*

*Before liming, you need to brush the wood hard in the direction of the grain. The paint must be extremely runny, and should be wiped off quickly, before it has time to dry.*

**Wax cleaner,** *for removing all the dirt and grease before liming*

**White spirit**

**Blue eggshell** *basecoat*

**Household brush** *for applying the oil colour*

**Coarse wire wool** *to rub down and soften the colour, and a wire brush to lift the wood grain*

**Clean cotton rag** *to use during the liming, for wiping off any excess colour*

**Masking tape and scalpel** *to use with the stencil, with a pencil for drawing the design*

**Large piece of stencil card** *with cut-out wreath and berry design for the top of the table*

**Oxide of Chromium, Prussian Blue and Indian Red oil colour** *with a small brush for the stencilling*

## METHOD

◆ If you wish to lime your piece of furniture, the liming must be done on bare wood. Paint on a thinned layer of colour (either oil- or water-based), and wipe it off with a rag until it is of the desired tone. The idea is for the grain of the wood to show through, and for the paint to adhere to the knots and crevices. If you prefer, lighten the wood using a proprietary brand of wood bleach instead.

◆ Make a suitable stencil for the top of your table, chest or chair, then cut it out and centre it on the surface. When you have positioned your stencil, keep it in place with some masking tape or a small amount of spray adhesive.

◆ Colour the stencil in the method of your choice, keeping the colours close in tone so as not to have them jarring. Additional detailing can be added to the sides or edges, using another stencil or part of your original one.

◆ Once dry, rub the stencilling with coarse wire wool to take away some of the freshness, if you wish.

First of all, I cleaned the table with wax cleaner to remove all traces of grease and dirt (soap and water works well too, if you leave it to dry before liming). Using a wire brush, I brushed hard in the direction of the wood grain to take out the soft grain on top. Then I limed the table with blue eggshell thinned with white spirit, and wiped it off before it was dry.

For the stencilling, I used Oxide of Chromium, Prussian Blue and Indian Red oil colour, which I applied with a small, coarse stencil brush. I added the same colour to the legs, but as there was still some varnish remaining, they are a slightly different colour to the top of the table. When the surface was dry, I rubbed the stencilled area with coarse wire wool to reduce the brightness.

*I designed my own stencils for this table, but if you do not feel confident enough to make your own, you can buy ready-made stencils. For the corners of the table, I used one stencil twice, reversing it to make a mirror image.*

*If you make a stencil, bear in mind that the blank areas are as important as the coloured areas. On the wreath stencil, virtually half of the design is not cut out, and these "bridges" hold the stencil together and form part of the design.*

# GILT-RUBBED CHAIR

THE DECORATION OF THIS elegant chair was really the most simple of all the techniques that I have done. My son's schoolteacher asked me to decorate the chair for her, having found it in her house when she moved there. Although she liked its shape, the chair was a little plain, so we decided to brighten it up with some gilding, using rub-on wax gilt cream.

Traditional gilding, using gold leaf, is difficult to do, but gilding with rub-on gilt cream is extremely easy, and the finished result can look stunning. My task was made even easier by the fact that this chair was already ebonized (painted black) when I decided to decorate it, so I did not have to apply a basecoat. All I needed to do was to fill in all the little carved scrolls, leaf shapes and dots with rub-on gilt cream. I chose an old gold with a hint of copper in it, which contrasts beautifully with the black paintwork (ebonized wood was a particular favourite in Victorian times). Some parts proved more tricky, so I used a small brush to poke into the finer areas, but for the rest of the chair, I simply dipped my little finger into the pot of gilt cream and rubbed it on, removing any excess from the surface with a rag.

If you have a chair with interesting carving, a little gilding can look surprisingly effective, particularly on a dark background. There are so many gilt creams available, that it is worth thinking carefully about the style of the piece and the result that you want to achieve before you begin to do any gilding. The old copper gold that I chose is typical of the Victorian era, and blends in well with the colours of the upholstery. A brassy lemon-coloured gold, on the other hand, would have done nothing to enhance the chair because it would have looked too modern. The finished effect looks rich and elegant, a far cry from the original plain black chair.

Copper gold          Old gold          Red gold          Orange gold

**Applying gilt to your furniture**
*Rub-on wax gilt cream, available in many tones, is easy to apply with your little finger, a brush or a soft cloth.*

I highlighted the carved detailing on the chair by applying rub-on wax gilt cream, which is extremely easy to use. There are various tones to choose from, ranging from silver through to gold. I chose a coppery-gold, rubbing it on with my little finger. To make certain that the gilt cream filled every corner, I also used a small paintbrush (an old toothbrush makes a handy tool for gilding, too).

As an alternative to gilt cream, I sometimes use gilt pencils, which are useful for intricate areas. For repairing scratches on furniture that is already gilded, a small amount of gilt filler can be softened in the fingers, then applied to the cracks, where it dries hard.

## METHOD

♦ Apply the basecoat of your choice and leave it to dry thoroughly. Eggshell paint is a good choice, since it is hard-wearing, and the finish that it produces is not too glossy, so it provides a good contrast with the gilding.

♦ You may need to apply several coats of paint, rubbing down between each layer with wet and dry sand-paper for a smooth finish.

♦ Select a suitable gilt cream for your piece of furniture. There are many colours available, ranging from a lemon-coloured modern gold to an old red gold, and also silver, pewter and copper colours too.

♦ Apply the gilt cream sparingly with your finger, rubbing it over the carved areas and into any grooves, wherever you wish. For tiny corners, use a very small brush dipped into the pot of gilt cream.

♦ Let this dry a little, then rub over the surface with a rag to remove all the excess gilt. Leave the gilt-rubbed surface to dry.

♦ To complete the look, use a soft cloth to buff the surface until it shines.

# DECORATIVE TECHNIQUES

# GLOSSARY OF PAINTING TERMS

Throughout the book, I have used a number of specialist terms with which you may be unfamiliar. This quick-reference glossary may be useful when you are uncertain about techniques, equipment or finishes.

**Acrylic paint** A fast-drying water-based paint with a waterproof finish.

**Ageing varnish** One of the two varnishes that are required for Cracklure (p.126).

**Arabesque** A decoration incorporating spirals and flourishes.

**Artist's brush** A small brush made of sable, squirrel, or nylon, used for delicate work.

**Artist's oil colour** Refined oil colour used by artists, and to make a *tinted glaze*.

**Badger hair brush** A softening brush for blending oil-based paints; used for Marbling (pp.114–117) and woodgraining (see Wood Finish pp.110–111). Available in various sizes.

**Basecoat** The first coat of paint for most of the decorative finishes.

**Bridges** The small areas on a stencil card that are not cut out, and serve to hold the whole design together.

**Chinoiserie** A style of decoration based on the imitation of Chinese motifs.

**Clear glaze** A mixture of linseed oil, dryers, whiting and other oils, which looks off-white in the can, and is used with oil colour and white spirit to make a *tinted glaze*. Other names are *transparent oil glaze* and *oil glaze*.

**Coach lining brush** The larger of the two specialist brushes used in Lining (p.104), to produce lines from ⅛-inch to 1-inch thick.

**Cracking varnish** One of the two varnishes used in Cracklure (p.126).

**Curlicue** A decorative twist.

**Découpage** The art of decorating furniture by sticking on paper cut-outs.

**Distressing** The technique of simulating signs of wear and tear on a painted surface.

**Eggshell** An oil-based paint with less sheen than gloss paint, often used as a *basecoat*.

**Emulsion** A water-based paint that can be used as a *basecoat*.

**Faux marbre** Imitation marble produced by the technique of Marbling (pp.114–117).

**Fitch** A bristle brush made of hog hair, used with oil colour in Marbling (pp.114–117). There are five different shapes.

**Flogging brush** A large, coarse, long-haired brush made of horse hair, used in Dragging (p.103).

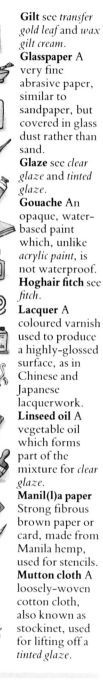

**Gilt** see *transfer gold leaf* and *wax gilt cream*.

**Glasspaper** A very fine abrasive paper, similar to sandpaper, but covered in glass dust rather than sand.

**Glaze** see *clear glaze* and *tinted glaze*.

**Gouache** An opaque, water-based paint which, unlike *acrylic paint*, is not waterproof.

**Hoghair fitch** see *fitch*.

**Lacquer** A coloured varnish used to produce a highly-glossed surface, as in Chinese and Japanese lacquerwork.

**Linseed oil** A vegetable oil which forms part of the mixture for *clear glaze*.

**Manil(l)a paper** Strong fibrous brown paper or card, made from Manila hemp, used for stencils.

**Mutton cloth** A loosely-woven cotton cloth, also known as stockinet, used for lifting off a *tinted glaze*.

**Oil colour** see *artist's oil colour*.

**Oil glaze** see *clear glaze*.

**Opaque** A coat of paint or a *tinted glaze* that is not transparent.

**Patina** The polished sheen characteristic of well-worn painted wood.

**Pigment** A coloured substance derived from plants, minerals and animals, mixed with water or oil to make paint.

**Primer** A sealer that is applied to bare wood before the *undercoat* and *basecoat*.

**Registration marks** Marks made in chalk or pencil, or nicks cut out of the corners of a stencil, to serve as positioning guides.

**Resin** A sticky gum secreted by the knots in wood.

**Rigger** A long-haired artist's brush, which can be used in Lining (p.104).

**Sable brush** A high-quality artist's brush made from the hair of the sable – a small arctic animal.

**Sealer** A protective coat of paint or *varnish* applied as an impenetrable layer before and/or after a decorative finish.

**Stippling brush** A large, stiff, rectangular bristle brush available in different sizes, used in Stippling (p.105) and other finishes.

**Stopping** A quick-drying, non-shrinking wood filler which dries hard.

**Swordliner** A tapered brush which holds a large amount of paint, used in Lining (p.104), to make long, continuous lines, and in Marbling (pp.114–117), to produce slightly broken, vein-like lines.

**Tinted glaze** The thin mixture of *clear glaze, oil colour* and *white spirit* used for many decorative finishes.

**Transfer gold leaf** Extremely thin sheets of gold, used in gilding as an alternative to *wax gilt cream*.

**Transparent oil glaze** see *clear glaze*.

**Turpentine** A clear oily liquid used as a solvent, or thinner for paints and varnishes. Also known as "turps", this should not be confused with *white spirit*.

**Turpentine substitute ("Turps")** A cheaper, inferior solvent, used for cleaning paint-brushes.

**Undercoat** An oil-based paint usually applied to wood after the *primer* and before the *basecoat*.

**Varnish** Different kinds of varnish are used for different purposes, such as Cracklure (p.126), lacquer-work, and for sealing painted surfaces. Clear polyurethane varnish produces a particularly hard-wearing surface, and is available in a matt, satin, eggshell, mid-sheen or gloss finish. Always use clear varnish.

**Veining** Part of the technique of Marbling (pp.114–117), requiring a *swordliner* or *rigger*.

**Water-based paints** Paints such as *emulsion, acrylic* and *gouache paint*.

**Wax cleaner** A liquid that safely removes old layers of wax, grease and dirt from painted surfaces.

**Wax gilt cream** Rub-on wax gilt cream, available in various tones of gold and silver, is often used to add highlights to carved areas.

**Wet and dry sandpaper** Sandpaper used in conjunction with water.

**White spirit** A clear liquid ingredient of a *tinted glaze*, also used as a solvent to clean brushes after using *oil colour* (not to be confused with *turpentine substitute*).

**Wire wool** An abrasive mass of fine or coarse wire, used for rubbing down rough surfaces.

**Woodworm** Furniture beetles lay eggs in the crevices of furniture, and the grubs later feed on the wood, boring small tunnels – the woodworm.

# DEFINING A COLOUR SCHEME

Furniture can either be painted in colours to match other furnishings around, or in styles to suit particular pieces. When choosing a colour scheme for your piece of furniture, try to concentrate on one or two main colours, with a few others acting as highlighters. With most painted finishes, the basecoat colour shows through in some parts, so choose your basecoat with care, since it plays as important a role as the tinted glaze in the finished design.

Here are some well-known colour schemes from around the world, many of which I have used as sources of inspiration for my painted furniture. You may find one or two of them useful in defining your own scheme.

▲ **Memphis**
*Bold colours and striking shapes suggest the Memphis style of contemporary furniture design. A few exciting,* *vibrant colours set against black and white, with some pastel shading, executed in characteristic geometrical shapes, can look stunning.*

▶ **Traditional Swedish**
*Deep greens and blues, and pinky terracotta, are traditional to Sweden and other parts of Northern Europe. They appear not only in classical Gustavian furniture, but also in more rustic pieces, and in the paintings of Carl Larsson.*

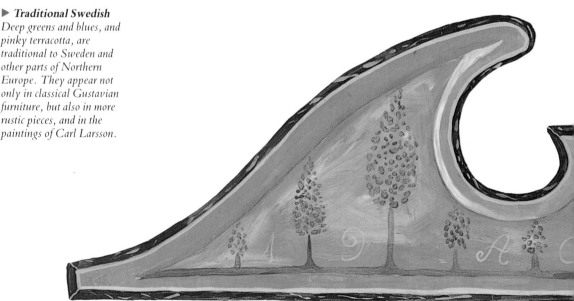

◀ **Omega Workshops**
The Omega Workshops, created by Roger Fry, Duncan Grant, Vanessa Bell and others, approached the decoration of furniture in a painterly way. Classical images painted in soft yellows, pinks and blue-greys played an important role in their schemes.

▲ **Early American**
Most American folk art is coloured in deep green, brick red, and buttermilk yellow. These were shades favoured by Scandinavian and German settlers, who used the same colours to decorate their barns and colour their quilt designs.

### ◀ Venetian and Georgian

Subtle and sophisticated colours were favoured by Venetian furniture-makers and their British counterparts. The most popular were a deep warm terracotta and a deep forest green, with highlights of Yellow Ochre, soft ivory and gold.

### ▲ Chinoiserie

There is probably no decorative style as distinctive as that of Oriental lacquerwork. The richly-coloured image of a pagoda or an exotic landscape, realized in gold, burnt orange and ivory on a black background is immediately identifiable.

# PREPARATION TECHNIQUES

### BARE WOOD

All bare wood, whether brand new or stripped of old paint, needs a coating of primer and undercoat before any other paint is applied, unless you wish to stencil directly on to the wood, or lime or bleach it. Before you apply either, however, rub down the surface with glasspaper or a power sander to ensure a smooth surface. Any cracks will need to be filled with filler or stopping, and any knots will need a coating of shellac to prevent resin staining the paintwork. To seal the pores in the wood and to provide a sound, stable base for the undercoat, apply a coat of primer. Then you can apply one or more coats of undercoat.

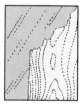

### PAINTED WOOD

You can work on furniture that is already painted if the paint is sound and smooth. Old gloss paint, if clean, can be covered directly, but new gloss paint may need to be keyed with glasspaper if you are applying a decorative covering. Some old paint can simply be peeled off the surface if it has been applied over old varnish. Old varnish will also need to be removed before any decorative paintwork can be done. If the varnish has lost its gloss you may be able to paint over it, but paint will not adhere to a shiny surface. If the surface has an old wax coating on it, you can remove this with wax cleaner.

Before applying any fresh paint to existing paintwork, the surface must be free from stains, dirt and dust. Otherwise, the new finish will look pimpled and will start to flake. You can remove surface dirt by brushing, washing or vacuuming. Any dust particles in awkward corners can be removed with a pointed object.

Use mild washing-up liquid and water, or soap and water to clean the surface, then rinse well. Make certain that the surface is dry before you apply any paint.

### STRIPPING OLD PAINT

Either heat or chemicals can be used to loosen old paint. Heat stripping is the most economical way of removing large areas of paint, but a blowlamp may scorch the surface unless it is handled expertly. A hot air gun can be directed at an area of paint and, after a few seconds, the paint will soften and you can peel it off with a scraper.

Chemical strippers are normally more suitable for furniture, and are particularly suitable for carved or moulded pieces and very thick, old paintwork. Peel-off stripper should be applied in a thick layer and left for several hours to eat through the layers of paint. Then it can be peeled off easily. Liquid stripper, which is effective on layers of varnish and one or two layers of paint, should be brushed on thickly with an old brush and can be scraped off after a few minutes. You may need to remove any remnants with wire wool and white spirit. Always wear gloves when working with a chemical stripper.

### MINOR REPAIRS

Dents, scratches and other minor damage may exist on an older piece of furniture. If you are worried about having the best possible surface and want to make your piece pristine, follow the directions below.

To raise a dent in solid wood, lay a damp cloth on it and then apply a heated soldering iron directly over the damage. The steam generated will swell the wood, pushing the crushed fibres back to their original level.

For small holes, as in woodworm, press melted wax scrapings into them using a knife or chisel blade. Then burnish with a piece of sandpaper. For large holes or cracks, press commercial stopper into the cavity with a palette knife until it stands proud. When set, finish off with fine sandpaper. When a repair is to be made to an unsupported edge use plastic wood. Using a knife blade, press it into place and shape it roughly to match the original contour. When set, sand flush.

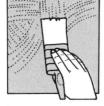

### APPLYING PAINT

If you are using an opened can, first make certain you have sufficient to cover the area. Before applying each coat, dust the surface with a lint-free rag to make sure no specks spoil the finish. Complete each surface in one session to prevent dried paint lines forming. You can normally brush emulsion and other water-based paint straight from the can without stirring if it is non-drip. Oil-based paint needs stirring and you may find it easier to pour it into a paint kettle. If it has already been opened, you may have to remove a skin. Score around the inside of the can and lift off the layer of solidified paint. Then stir thoroughly. Before you put your brush into the paint, flick the bristles to dislodge dust and any loose bristles.

Gloss paint is trickier to apply than emulsion. For a smooth, shiny finish without brush marks and runs, do not overload the brush. Dip the brush into the paint, not too deeply, and squeeze off excess on the inside of the paint kettle. Cover a small area with two or three strokes applied in the direction of the wood grain. Then change direction and spread the paint lightly to cover the surface. Work back again with the grain, finishing with an upward stroke. Reload the

brush and, leaving a gap the width of the brush, move on to paint a parallel strip. Then paint across to fill in the area between strips. At the join, to avoid a thick ridge forming at each overlap, allow the brush tips to gently skim the line. Finally, brush vigorously over the whole area and finish off with vertical strokes. Do not expect the first coat to cover the surface perfectly. The paint must look thin. Let the piece dry for several hours until it is no longer tacky, sanding with fine-grade glasspaper after each coat.

If you are working with non-drip emulsion paint, stir it thoroughly, then coat your brush with a generous layer of paint and apply in horizontal bands. Work quickly and conceal the joins before the paint dries. Finish off matt emulsion with criss-cross strokes; silk or satin emulsion with light, upward strokes.

## A USEFUL TIP

Cleaning your brushes can be quite a chore if they are covered with oil paint. Here is a useful tip:
♦ Before you use a new brush, bore a hole through the base of the handle, in the centre.
♦ When you need to clean your brush, push a long nail through the hole, and balance it on the top of a jam jar containing brush-cleaning fluid.
♦ The brush will remain suspended in the jam jar, which can be left standing without spoiling the shape of the brush.

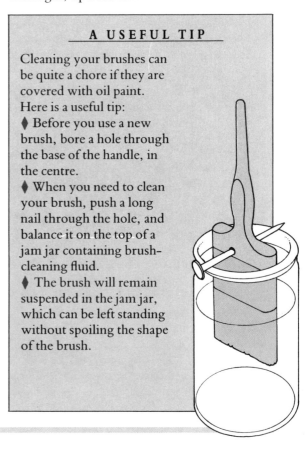

## TINTED GLAZE MIXTURE

The tinted glaze mixture required for most finishes is usually made up of the following: 50% clear glaze, 50% white spirit and as much artist's oil colour as you need to achieve the depth of colour that you want for your particular finish. The checklists accompanying each painting technique advise you if you need more white spirit or oil colour than usual. For blues, it is essential to use white eggshell with the glaze (up to a third of your total amount).

The tinted glaze should be applied thinly, and therefore dries quite quickly, especially in a warm temperature. The basecoat should still show through once you have applied the glaze. The first five minutes in which the glaze starts to dry is when it is time to sponge, dab or mutton-cloth over the surface.

The glaze remains soluble in white spirit for quite a long time, so any splashes on the walls or floor can be wiped off with a little white spirit.

If you have to leave the work half done overnight, always cover any glaze mixture with cling film, to prevent dust from settling on the surface. The cling film will also prevent too much moisture loss, and stops a thick skin forming on the surface. A thick skin can be removed, but if it becomes lumpy for any reason, these lumps can be removed by straining the glaze through a mutton cloth, a sieve or some nylon tights.

## BRUSH CARE

When working with oil-based paint, it is essential to clean the brushes well in order to keep them in good condition. Most brushes become more flexible as they get older, but new ones are quite stiff and more difficult to clean, and often shed a few hairs when you first start using them. The general rule for brush care is to clean the brush well in commercial brush cleaner or white spirit, wash it thoroughly in a solution of washing-up liquid and water, then rinse and allow it to dry. This is particularly important with higher-priced brushes.

**Flogging brush** *Clean first in white spirit or brush cleaner, then in washing-up liquid and water. To retain shape, keep wrapped in paper and store lying down.*

**Fitch** *Simply clean the brush in white spirit until all the glaze has been removed.*

**Swordliner** *Clean in white spirit, then washing-up liquid and water. Wipe a little petroleum jelly on the brush to reshape, and store the brush away carefully.*

**Varnishing brush** *Simply rinse well in white spirit to remove the varnish.*

**Artist's brush** *Clean in white spirit, then rinse well in water. Use a little petroleum jelly to help retain its shape.*

**Combs** *Wipe with a rag and white spirit. Never leave combs in white spirit.*

**Sponges** *Clean in white spirit, then washing-up liquid and water. Leave to dry naturally.*

**Mutton cloths and rags** *These are a dangerous fire risk if left lying around covered in oil glaze. Leave rags to dry naturally by hanging them out, and never leave them in a heap.*

**Household brush** *Clean well with white spirit or brush cleaner. This can be left in white spirit for short periods.*

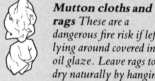

**Softening brush** *Wash gently with white spirit or brush cleaner before and after use. Clean in washing-up liquid and water, rolling the brush in your hands to remove the water.*

**Stippling brush** *Clean thoroughly after use. Never let the glaze dry on the brush, or leave the brush standing in glaze or white spirit.*

# SPONGING ON

SPONGING ON is one of the simplest and quickest techniques, producing an informal speckled effect. It is also one of the few finishes that can be done successfully using either an oil-based glaze or water-based emulsion. Oil glazes have greater depth; emulsion coats are opaque. All you need is a soft open-holed sponge (a natural sea sponge is ideal). The method is simply to dip the sponge into your glaze or paint and pat it over the surface.

Sponging on is suitable for most pieces of furniture, but is not so successful on intricate or carved articles. For furniture, a small sponge is best. If there are any tricky corners, either squeeze the sponge or break a small piece off.

When sponging on, the first step is to paint the item with an eggshell basecoat in the colour of your choice. When this is dry, sponge on another tone or a different colour, bearing in mind that similar tones will give a soft effect while strong contrasts can look rather crude. You can also sponge on more than one coat. Either apply one colour at a time when the previous one has dried, or, using two sponges, apply one colour on top of another while still wet, so that the two colours merge. The final layer is always the strongest in tone.

Stand back and view your work at regular intervals so that you can see how even the effect is. If you do make mistakes, glaze can be wiped off with a little white spirit on a rag, and emulsion paint with water.

The sponge should always be softened in clean water before use. If you put a little tinted glaze into a paint tray, you can dip the sponge into it without allowing it to become soaked. The effect is spoiled if the sponge is saturated with glaze. You may need to rinse out the sponge in white spirit (or water for emulsion) during use if it becomes too sticky, and always clean the sponge well after use.

**MATERIALS**
- Eggshell basecoat
- Tinted glaze (see also p.99):
  clear glaze (45%)
  white spirit (55%)
  oil colour (amount to suit) or,
- Emulsion or acrylic paints
- Sponge
- Paint tray

▲ *Pour a little tinted glaze into a paint tray, and dip a moistened sponge lightly into it. Use emulsion straight from the can.*

▲ *Pat the lightly coated sponge over the surface, varying the pressure if you wish, creating an even overall pattern.*

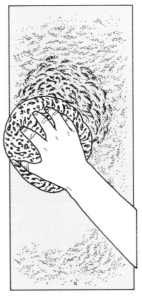

◄ *Applying two or more tones using different sponges produces a greater impression of depth. The second colour can be applied while the first is still wet, which will make the tones merge somewhat, but mistakes cannot be rectified. By allowing your first coat to dry, mistakes with the second coat can be simply wiped off. Keep the colours close in tone to produce a soft finish. The last colour that you apply will be the most dominant, so consider your colour range carefully. If you want to create a strong contrast, apply a darker basecoat with lighter tones on top.*

# SPONGING OFF

SPONGING OFF produces a cloudy or speckled effect. It is a little more difficult than sponging on, involving several stages, but can be done successfully on all types of furniture. The method is to apply an eggshell basecoat and let it dry, then to brush on an oil-based glaze or emulsion paint, and finally, to sponge it off, revealing the colour of the basecoat.

By varying the dabbing action slightly, the effect can be as soft or hard as you like. An impression of depth is achieved if you sponge off first, allow the surface to dry, then sponge on in the colour of the basecoat, particularly if you use dark colours and a gloss varnish.

Concentrate on small areas at a time, so that you can work through the stages without the glaze becoming too tacky and impossible to work with. Try to begin sponging off within about five minutes of applying glaze, and sooner for emulsion (the drying time will vary depending on room temperature). It is important to give the surface as uniform a covering as possible to achieve an even result. Excess glaze or paint can then be removed from the surface with a small household brush.

**MATERIALS**
- Eggshell basecoat
- Tinted glaze (see also p.99):
  clear glaze (45%)
  white spirit (55%)
  oil colour (amount to suit) or,
- Emulsion
- Household brush (size according to size of object)
- Paint tray
- Sponge

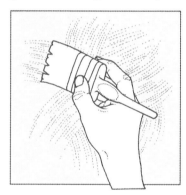

◀ *Cover the dry eggshell basecoat evenly with a thin coat of tinted glaze or some emulsion, using a household brush. Always try to concentrate on small areas at a time, in order to keep the glaze workable.*

◀ *Dab the moistened sponge over the surface to lift the glaze and produce the speckled effect. When the sponge becomes sticky with glaze, clean it in white spirit and washing-up liquid, rinsing it thoroughly.*

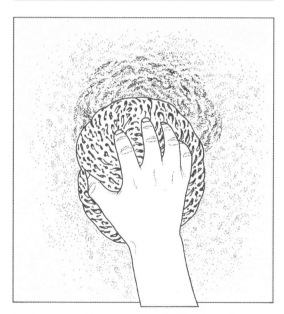

▲ *To vary the effect, try using more than one colour, either applying the glazes over one another while still wet, or leaving each glaze to dry first. Experiment with using a little or a lot of pressure with the sponge, until you create the finish that you want.*

# COLOURWASHING

COLOURWASHING's effect depends upon whether a cloth or a brush is used to wipe off the glaze. The effect with the cloth is much softer than the effect produced with the brush. The technique is quite straightforward, and involves painting a thin layer of tinted glaze over an eggshell basecoat, then wiping it off with a brush or cloth in large sweeping strokes.

Colourwashing is really only suitable for large objects because the effect is so loose, and is best confined to dining-table tops, wardrobes and cupboards. It can also work well in the panels of a cupboard, with dragged surrounds to keep the look well-defined. Colourwashing also disguises imperfections quite well, and on uneven surfaces, gives a slightly distressed effect of paint rubbed and worn with age.

The finish is best when the surface is brushed or wiped when still tacky to leave only a thin layer of glaze. A stronger effect can be achieved using dark basecoats with darker colours or tones on top. Once the first layer is dry, others can be brushed on. A final gloss varnish will produce a mock lacquer finish.

**MATERIALS**
- Eggshell basecoat
- Tinted glaze (see also p.99):
  clear glaze (45%)
  white spirit (55%)
  oil colour
  (amount to suit)
- Wallpaper brush or other large brush
- Paint tray
- Gloss varnish
- Cotton rag

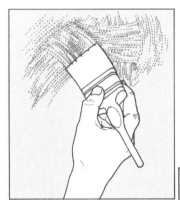

◄ *Apply a thin layer of tinted glaze on to the dry eggshell-covered surface, brushing it on very thinly. Using a large brush, such as a wallpaper brush, and working in large sweeping strokes, wipe the glaze off.*

► *Alternatively, in order to achieve an effect that is cloudy and soft, use a dry cotton rag to wipe off the glaze.*

◄ *Once dry, another colour or tone can be applied on top of the first layer.*

# DRAGGING

▲ *With a household brush, working vertically, apply a thin layer of tinted glaze over the dry eggshell-covered surface.*

**MATERIALS**
- ◆ Eggshell basecoat
- ◆ Tinted glaze (see also p.99):
  clear glaze (45%)
  white spirit (55%)
  oil colour (amount to suit)
- ◆ Spray varnish
- ◆ Household brush (size according to size of object)
- ◆ Flogging brush (2½″ is suitable for most furniture)
- ◆ Cotton rag
- ◆ Paint tray

▲ *Alternatively, on small objects, you can use a rag dipped into the glaze, and drag it down the surface.*

THE TECHNIQUE OF DRAGGING produces fine, subtle lines that give furniture elegance and an impression of height. It is essential that the surface is smooth, as every bump or crack shows through once the surface has been painted.

Various brushes can be used, including the traditional dragging brush (giving a loose, well-covered grainy look), a flogging brush which gives a well-defined and thinner cover), and finally the well-worn household brush, which can be quite delicate, especially on a small piece of furniture such as a bedside table. Always brush in the direction of the grain. On small table tops, a rag dipped in the glaze works quite well too if you pull it over the surface. To finish, use a spray varnish, since it does not spoil the thin layer of colour, whereas a brush and varnish may do.

To achieve the best results, it is important that the tones of the eggshell basecoat and glaze are close, in order to produce the variegated finish characteristic of dragging. If there is a great difference in tone, the result will be too stripy. It is therefore not a good idea to use a white basecoat unless your glaze is a very light colour. When using a flogging brush, as the brush becomes overloaded, flick the glaze off and wipe it on a rag. Paint the glaze on extremely thinly, keeping it out of the edges and corners to avoid a build-up. Too much glaze on the brush will also spoil the subtle effect.

▲ *Drag the flogging brush vertically over the surface with enough pressure to produce lines. On wooden objects, always follow the grain of the wood.*

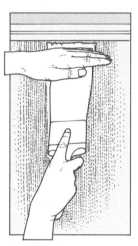

▲ *To avoid unattractive lines where the brush marks join, go over these areas again with a gliding action, increasing the pressure slowly as you go. Finish with a spray varnish.*

# LINING

LINES ADDED TO FURNITURE can enhance its shape, improve a dull, flat surface, and give an impression of shape and elegance. The colors used can be either a lighter or darker tone, or even a total contrast to the background color. The hand-painted line is the most beautiful, as it is softly wavering and natural. On old pieces of furniture, the irregularity of these hand-painted lines gives character and charm to the piece. The most simple method is to paint a single line around a table top or drawer front, following the edge. If the object has been varnished already, you can use masking tape as a guide to help you paint in a straight line. This gives a solid line of color and is best done when a wide line is required. Take care, as masking tape can bend easily, to make certain that the lines are straight. Masking tape is available in various widths, so you can come in from the edge as little or as much as you wish.

Alternatively, you can use a lining brush. These brushes hold a large amount of glaze, allowing for a long flow without the need to reload the brush. They are a little difficult to use skilfully, and require a steady hand. There are various types of lining brushes. A swordliner has a short handle with hairs which come to a fine point. Coach lining brushes come in various lengths and thicknesses, and their main feature is that they are long. The wooden part acts as an anchor and the hairs are like a tail which follows behind loaded with glaze.

The consistency of the glaze should be relatively thin so that it flows freely from the brush. The harder you press on the surface, the wider the line will be. It is essential to use your little finger as a guide, resting it on the surface edge to help you to paint in a straight line. Once your hand is in position, keep it stiff and then pull it down quickly to make the line. The secret of a straight line is not to look at the brush, but rather, to look where the line is going to be, giving yourself enough room to make a long sweep with the brush. Make the line longer than necessary, then wipe off the ends with a soft cloth before the glaze dries.

Lastly, you can use a waterproof felt-tipped pen with a ruler. This gives a fine precise line.

**MATERIALS**
- Oil color (amount to suit) mixed with white oil paint
- Artist's brush and
- Masking tape or,
- Swordliner or coach lining brush or,
- Felt-tipped pen and ruler
- Clean cotton rag

▲ *Load your lining brush with glaze and try to complete the line all in one go, keeping your hand steady by using your little finger as a guide.*

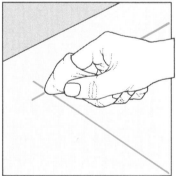

▲ *If you require a thicker line, simply increase the pressure on the surface. Wipe off any excess glaze where the lines meet before they dry.*

# STIPPLING

STIPPLING produces a delicate speckled finish that appears flat when viewed from a distance, but up close gives a surface a feeling of depth. It looks very good on carved objects and moldings. Pastel colors look impressionistic, while bright colors are bold and striking. Stippling shows up any defects on furniture, so it is best to use this technique only on furniture with smooth surfaces, or alternatively, fill any dents before you start to stipple.

Stippling requires a steady hand to produce a pleasing result, and has to be done using a stippling brush, which is a very costly item. A similar technique can be achieved using a mutton cloth, although a large area viewed from a distance will look cloudy. Generally you need more oil color than the usual amount for the glaze mixture, and the glaze should be applied very thinly with a household brush. The stippling brush is then used to spread the paint evenly, obliterating all the brush marks. When the glaze is almost dry, any excess can be removed from the corners and edges with a smaller stippling brush.

**MATERIALS**
- Eggshell basecoat
- Tinted glaze (see also p.99):
  clear glaze (45%)
  mineral spirit (55%)
  oil color (to suit)
- Stippling brushes (suitable sizes: 4" × 1", 3" × 4" or 2" × 6")
- Clean cotton rag
- Paint tray

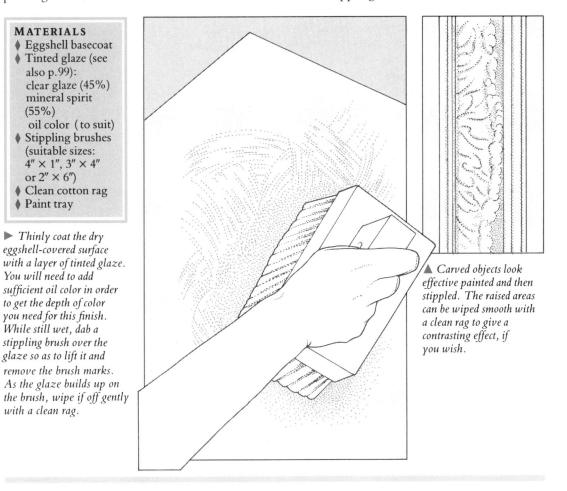

▶ *Thinly coat the dry eggshell-covered surface with a layer of tinted glaze. You will need to add sufficient oil color in order to get the depth of color you need for this finish. While still wet, dab a stippling brush over the glaze so as to lift it and remove the brush marks. As the glaze builds up on the brush, wipe if off gently with a clean rag.*

▲ *Carved objects look effective painted and then stippled. The raised areas can be wiped smooth with a clean rag to give a contrasting effect, if you wish.*

# RAGGING

RAGGING is an easy, adaptable, quick technique, requiring no special tools, that produces a dappled decorative finish. Ragging effects range from the soft and subtle to the sharp and bold, depending on the colours, the types of rag used, and for how long you dab. The method of working is to paint a very thin tinted glaze over an eggshell basecoat using a household brush, removing the glaze afterwards with bunched-up rags. Soft cloths or rags (for example, old cotton sheets and T-shirts), dabbed on an area many times produce a hazy-edged design, while a crisper heavy fabric dabbed once or twice makes a large pattern with a sharper edge. Do not use nylon fabrics for ragging, as they do not absorb glaze.

Ragging works well on its own or as a background to stencilling, and is most successful on larger pieces of furniture. On small pieces of furniture, keep the tones very close indeed. A larger item can generally take a greater depth of tone. Usually no brush marks are left visible but you may like to leave some showing to give a contrasting look. Two or more colours applied in separate coats create a greater feeling of depth, particularly since you begin with a pale coat and paint a slightly darker tone on top, as with all paint effects.

| MATERIALS | |
|---|---|
| ◆ Eggshell basecoat | ◆ Household brush |
| ◆ Tinted glaze (see also p.99): clear glaze (50%) white spirit (50%) oil colour (amount to suit) | (size according to size of object) |
| | ◆ Cotton rag or non-nylon rag (or, brown paper or plastic bag) |
| ◆ Small stippling brush | ◆ Paint tray |

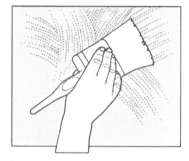

▶ Evenly cover the dry eggshell-painted surface with a thin layer of tinted glaze, using a household brush.

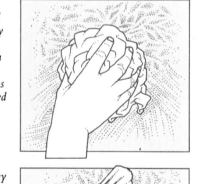

▶ Using a loosely crumpled cotton rag, gently lift off the glaze before it has been allowed to dry. Re-fold the rag as it becomes covered with glaze. A new rag may be needed occasionally when the existing one becomes too sticky to use.

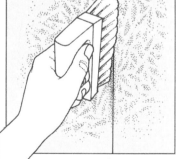

▶ To remove any excess build-up of glaze in the corners and along the edges, use a small stippling brush or a small household brush.

## BAGGING

Crumpled brown paper or plastic bags with an extra-thin glaze can be used but as no glaze is absorbed, the effect is to create thick areas of glaze in parts. Blot the bag on kitchen paper to remove excess glaze, and renew only if it becomes soggy; the crazy-paving effect is more consistent if you use only one bag.

# RAG ROLLING

RAG ROLLING is a combination of ragging and stippling, in which you brush on a tinted glaze, stipple it, then rag roll it. These stages must be done quite speedily so that the glaze does not become too dry to work with. An effective area for rag rolling is on the panels of a cupboard, with the rest of the cupboard dragged (see p.103) or stippled (see p.105).

Once the furniture has been stippled, the rag rolling may be either light or heavy, depending on the result desired. The rag can be folded into a sausage shape, but this makes one definite pattern of several horizontal lines. The usual method is to crumple the rag and roll it over the surface like a rolling pin. The idea is to create an even texture, which depends on distributing the glaze evenly with the stippling brush. Stippling on top of rag rolling gives you quite a different effect. On very small areas you can lightly rag over the area with a dabbing motion as in ragging. You will need a fair amount of oil colour because the stippling action removes much of the colour. Always keep the colour of the glaze and basecoat close in tone. To remove excess glaze, use a stippling brush once the glaze has had time to dry. If the glaze is too dry to work with, apply more pressure with the stippling brush.

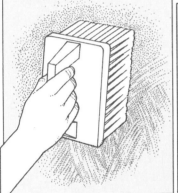

▲ *Apply the tinted glaze over a dry eggshell basecoat as you would for ragging (see opposite), taking care not to apply the glaze too thickly. Then, using a stippling brush suitable for the size of the furniture you are working on, stipple over the surface evenly.*

**MATERIALS**
♦ Eggshell basecoat
♦ Tinted glaze (see also p.99):
  clear glaze (45%)
  white spirit (55%)
  oil colour (more than usual)
♦ Stippling brush (size according to size of object)
♦ Household brush (size according to size of object)
♦ Paint tray
♦ Cotton rags

◀ *Before the glaze has completely dried, roll a crumpled-up rag or cloth across the tacky surface, taking care not to smudge the stippled glaze by letting the rag slip and slide over the surface. Remember always to crumple the rag rather than fold it.*

# COMBING

COMBING is an ancient decorative technique; the effect produced is stripy, as the glaze is lifted off where the teeth of the comb touch the surface. You can create a variety of patterns on most surfaces, particularly if you use several colours and different-sized combs, and work in more than one direction. If the surface is rough, the comb may miss areas and the finish will not be consistent, but if it is too smooth, the comb may slip and slide about, so fill any dents or scratches before you start.

Various combs are available to buy, usually quite small, made of metal or rubber. Metal combs should be covered with a piece of cotton rag to prevent scratching. They produce a grainy look or one of a series of stripes. Alternatively, it is quite simple to make your own comb, cut from cardboard or a cork tile, which will not scratch the surface. For large areas, a wide one helps you to cover the surface more easily.

Before you start combing, apply a light-coloured eggshell basecoat over the surface. With small objects, it is best then to go over the surface with a mutton cloth when it is still tacky to remove the brush marks. When combing, it is important to consider the combination of colours and tones, since the final layer of glaze will be the most dominant. If you make mistakes and wish to remove them, allow the surface to dry, then apply more glaze and start combing again.

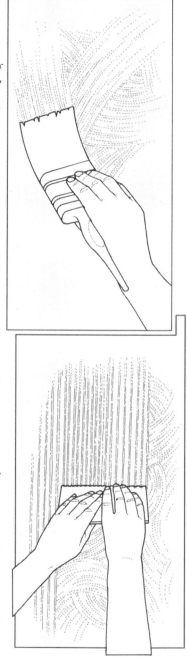

▶ *Make certain your surface is fairly smooth, because if it is too bumpy the comb will miss areas. If necessary, fill any dents or scratches first, and sand the surface with fine sandpaper until smooth. Apply a light-coloured eggshell basecoat with a household brush, then if you wish, remove the brush marks with a mutton cloth while the glaze is still tacky.*

▶ *When the basecoat is thoroughly dry, apply a thin layer of glaze, and comb across the surface, working vertically or horizontally to make the pattern of your choice (see Alternative patterns, opposite). The teeth lift off the glaze where they touch the surface, and if the comb is home-made with unequal teeth, you can vary the pattern by turning the comb around as you go.*

## MATERIALS

- ♦ Eggshell basecoat
- ♦ Tinted glaze (see p.99):
  clear glaze (50%)
  white spirit (50%)
  oil colour (amount to suit)
- ♦ Mutton cloth
- ♦ Household brush
- ♦ Rubber, metal or homemade combs (requiring cardboard or cork tiles and scissors)
- ♦ Paint tray
- ♦ Cotton rag

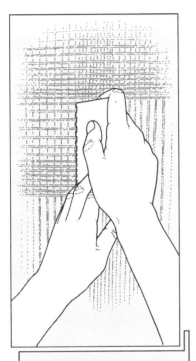

◀ *To create a chequered pattern, comb the surface vertically first, then horizontally, or vice versa. Wipe any excess glaze off the comb, so as not to make blobs or ridges on the combed surface.*

◀ *Another idea is to make wavy or zig-zag lines, using small or large combs, or a combination of both, working in different directions. Remember always to wipe excess glaze off the comb with a rag as you work, and clean the comb with white spirit once you have finished.*

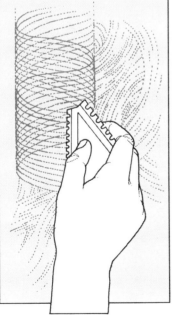

## ALTERNATIVE PATTERNS

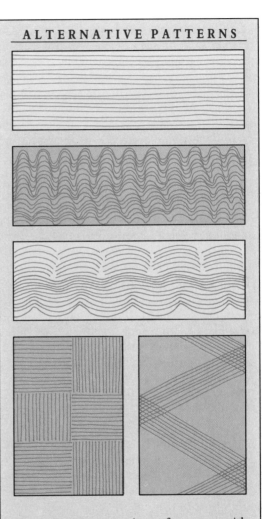

You can create a variety of patterns with combing, using different-sized combs and a selection of colours. Experiment by making an assortment of wide and narrow combs out of card or cork tiles, with equal or unequal gaps between the teeth. Use these to comb wavy lines, zig-zags, criss-crosses, scallops and basketweave. The finished effect can look stunning.

# WOOD FINISH

A REALISTIC MOCK WOOD effect is one of the most difficult finishes to master. Before you embark on woodgraining, study the characteristics of a piece of real wood. The most important aspect of woodgraining is the colour and tonal quality. You should match your eggshell basecoat with the lightest colour of your chosen wood, and try to make the glaze match the darker colour of the wood, keeping glaze and basecoat close in tone.

Wood finishes can be reproduced in both water- and oil-based paints. Some finishes look better in water-based paints, some in oil-based paints, a few being a combination. Often wood can be painted with an oil-based glaze, with the graining being done in water-based paints.

The simpler graining techniques use oil glazes. An eggshell basecoat is painted on, then overgraining is done with a transparent oil glaze. Simple woodgrain finishes include pine, oak and mahogany; birdseye maple and burr walnut are more difficult. The latter two look more successful with water-based paints.

The maple finish illustrated here was used on the wood-finish bed featured in the book. A more complicated finish is to add the "bird's eyes". This is achieved by making random dots or "eyes" with your knuckle or finger while the glaze is wet. The colour is lifted off, leaving white-ringed spots which can be softened with a badger-hair brush, by dragging downwards.

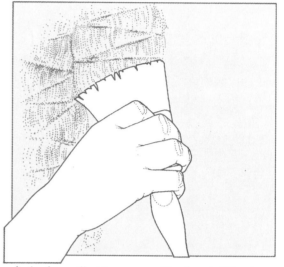

▲ *Apply an off-white or cream eggshell basecoat; allow it to dry completely, then apply a tinted glaze* *with a household brush, wiggling the brush across the surface with a jerking motion.*

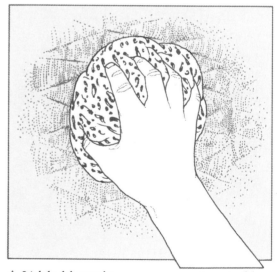

▲ *Lightly dab over the surface with a sponge, to give a speckled broken* *appearance to parts of the graining. This results in a plain maple finish.*

**MATERIALS**
- Off-white or cream eggshell basecoat
- Tinted glaze (see also p.99):
  clear glaze (50%)
  white spirit (50%)
  oil colour (amount to suit)
- Household brush (size according to size of object)
- Softening brush
- Sponge
- Fine sable brush or conté crayon
- Paint tray

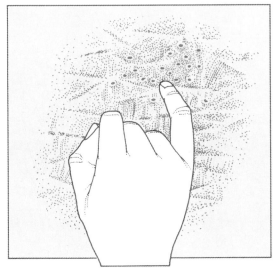

▲ For birdseye maple, while the glaze is still wet, gently dab your fingertip or knuckle over the surface to simulate the "eyes" in the wood grain.

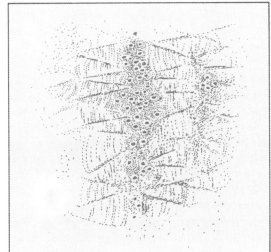

▲ The mock birdseye maple wood finish will look effective and can be left as it is at this stage, then varnished once the surface has dried completely.

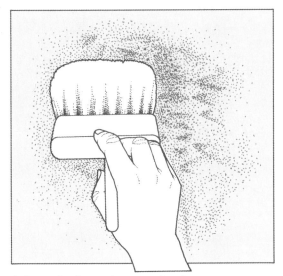

▲ Leave the glaze to dry, or if you prefer, soften the effect with a softening brush when the wet spots are nearly dry, dabbing them downwards.

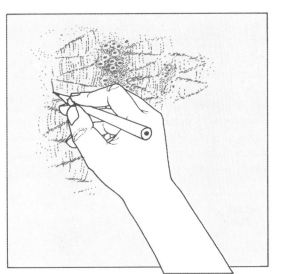

▲ Alternatively, you can overgrain it with a sable brush and a little oil colour, or using a conté crayon, draw around the contours of the "eyes".

# SPATTERING

SPATTERING is not as easy as some of the other techniques because it requires a firm, steady hand and quite a degree of control. The idea is to load your brush with tinted glaze and, by tapping the handle of the brush with a stick, to flick the glaze over the dry eggshell basecoat to produce a speckled smattering of colour. This effect is suitable for picture and mirror frames that might look heavy if treated with brushed-on glazes. It is also an easy way to apply texture to a plain painted surface.

With smaller objects, it is best to use a small bristle brush, and to tap the handle with your finger, so that you have greater control over the glaze. This will produce a light fine splattering of colour rather than unattractive blobs of paint. Too much thick glaze on the brush causes blobs, and too thin a mixture makes the glaze run and merge so that you lose the speckled look. If this happens, you can wipe the glaze off and start again. It is always a good idea to test the consistency of the glaze first, and to check that the brush is not overloaded. When choosing colours and tones, take care to avoid a frenzy of colour by choosing too broad a range. Instead, limit your colours and tones to two or three that complement each other, and always test them first with your brush on a piece of card. Colours of the same intensity, when viewed from a distance will cancel each other out and appear neutral.

◀ Once the eggshell basecoat has dried off completely, mask off around the area that you are going to work on, using masking tape. Always protect the surrounding area in case you flick some of the tinted glaze on to the table or floor. For the spattering, use a hoghair fitch brush.

▶ When working on small objects, the glaze should be thin enough to run when rubbed against the edge of the paint tray. It is then sufficiently runny to spatter when the handle of the brush is tapped with another brush handle. You may find that you have more control if you tap the brush with your finger instead.

---

### MATERIALS

- Eggshell basecoat
- Tinted glaze (see also p.99):
  clear glaze (50%)
  white spirit (50%)
  oil colour (amount to suit)
- Paint tray
- Hoghair fitch brush (size according to size of object)
- Another brush handle or a stick
- Masking tape
- White spirit
- Small bristle brush

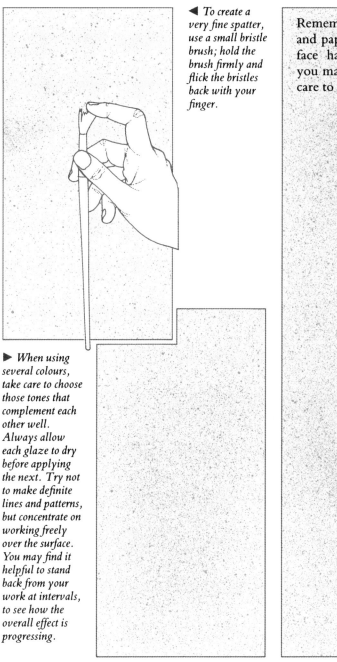

◀ *To create a very fine spatter, use a small bristle brush; hold the brush firmly and flick the bristles back with your finger.*

▶ *When using several colours, take care to choose those tones that complement each other well. Always allow each glaze to dry before applying the next. Try not to make definite lines and patterns, but concentrate on working freely over the surface. You may find it helpful to stand back from your work at intervals, to see how the overall effect is progressing.*

Remember to remove the masking tape and paper only when your spattered surface has dried completely. Otherwise, you may smudge the areas that you took care to protect from splashes.

# MARBLING

MARBLING is a very old technique, and the effects produced vary widely in their colour and pattern. Once you have found a marble that you like, you can use it as a reference for your own interpretation. It is best to marble surfaces which would, in reality be marble, although there are some lovely folk pieces that have marbling on the drawer fronts, and marbled baths are popular, too. Since there are many different methods of marbling, it is wise to experiment with the technique on a spare piece of hardboard first.

When marbling, the technique is to lay a glaze over an off-white eggshell base, then to distress the surface while the glaze is still wet, and finally to add veining after the glaze has dried. You need not do all three stages, since the marbling looks effective at every stage. The most difficult part is the veining. If you allow the surface to dry first, you can wipe the veining off and start again if it is not successful without spoiling the work already done.

The most suitable pieces of furniture for marbling are those that have large, flat surfaces, such as tables and washstands. Carved areas are more difficult to deal with. It is most essential to keep colour and direction in mind as you work, taking care not to overwork the shapes or have too many contrasting tones going in different directions. Natural marbles are usually veined in one direction, and the colours are quite subtle and gentle.

## MATERIALS

- ♦ Eggshell basecoat
- ♦ Tinted glaze (see also p.99): clear glaze (55%) white spirit (45%) oil colour (amount to suit)
- ♦ Mutton cloth
- ♦ Fitches (sizes according to size of object)
- ♦ Softening brush and small bristle brush
- ♦ Rags/newspapers/cling film/sponge/feathers
- ♦ Stippling brush (for carved items only)
- ♦ Rigger and sword-liner or sable brush

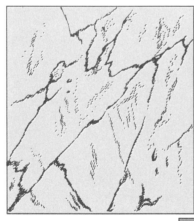
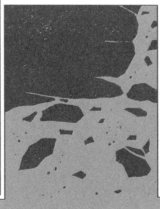
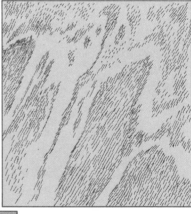

## MARBLE TYPES

**White Marble** has a white basecoat, with a hint of blue. Over this are light tones of greeny- and yellowy-grey.

**Black and Gold Marble** is veined in Yellow Ochre and Indian Red, with finer lines and gold transfer leaf added.

**Sienna Marble** has a dead white basecoat, with Raw Sienna and white on top, and veining in Raw Umber, Raw Sienna and white.

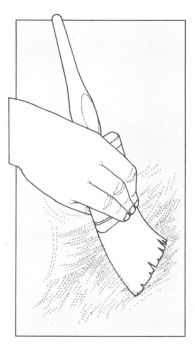

◀ *Coat the surface with eggshell to provide a good foundation. An off-white mixture is better than dead white. Once the basecoat has dried, it may need a light sanding to produce the smooth, flat surface that is characteristic of marble.*

▶ *Next, add the tinted glaze, working from the paint tray and mixing the colours as you go. Begin by applying a middle tone of glaze in a diagonal direction, using your fitch brush. Then, using a different fitch, apply a darker tone, casually and without attempting an even texture, working in the same direction as before, as if the area were part of a much larger piece of marble, without any definite edges.*

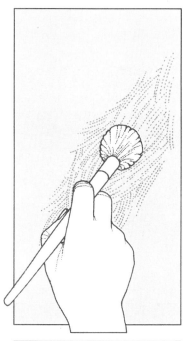

◀ *As you work, begin to wipe off some areas of glaze with a dry bristle brush where you want the lighter areas to be. Alternatively, add a little white, keeping the colours close in tone, and the general look soft, with a gentle gradation of tone. Using a mutton cloth, remove all brush marks, dabbing the darker patches.*

▶ *With a badger hair softening brush, go over the surface, blending the effect a little. If you are working on a carved object, use a stippling brush to obliterate the brush marks and leave the colours. Once this is done, you can leave the marbling as it is, or proceed to add further effects by distressing and veining.*

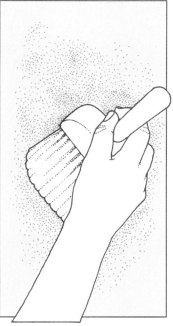

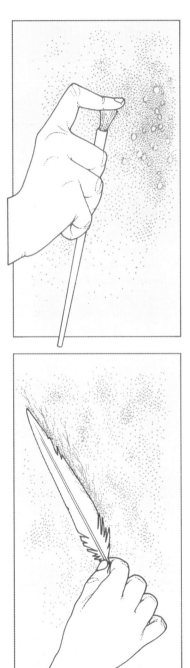

◀ If you wish, you can distress the surface by flicking white spirit over it with a small clean brush to break up the glaze. After a few seconds, this will produce flecks of white. It is best to test the brush before flicking the white spirit, so as not to overdo the effect. The distressing techniques shown opposite may give you some ideas.

◀ Once the surface has been distressed, you can add veining using a swordliner, a sable brush or goose feathers. Always use tones similar to those used for the marbling, working in the same direction as the marble. If you work on a dry surface, it will be easier to remove your mistakes by wiping the glaze off. Cross-veining is difficult to do well, and you need to be quite skilful to achieve a successful result. Alternatively, you can do veining using white spirit on a small brush, which will remove the colour where you "paint".

## USING CLING FILM

While the glaze is still tacky, apply small pieces of cling film to some areas. Blow on it, then lift it off. This will remove areas of glaze in irregular-shaped patches. Do this when the glaze has dried a little rather than when it is wet, or the patterns will be too extreme. Once this is done, you can use the softening brush to blend the marbling a little, and remove hard lines, or stipple the surface to vary the effect. A rather different finish can be achieved by twisting the cling film, then laying it on the surface diagonally in the same direction as the marble.

## SPONGING ON

Wet a natural sponge, squeeze out the water, then dip it into a mixture of white spirit (45%), clear glaze (55%), and sufficient oil colour. Sponge lightly over the surface, so that the marbling still shows through. Once the glaze has become tacky, soften the effect slightly with a softening or stippling brush. If the glaze is too wet, you will take off too much colour. You can also use pure white spirit on the sponge, dabbing lightly to remove parts of the colour in an uneven, blotchy way.

## RAGGING

Another idea is to use a scrunched-up rag or a newspaper to "distress" the marbled surface a little. As with sponging, you will need to test the surface to see how wet the glaze is first. The wetter the glaze, the greater the effect.

## HITTING THE SURFACE

This is an effective, fun, and simple way to distress the marbled surface. With a long, dry rag, hit the surface diagonally in the same direction as the pattern of marble while the glaze is still quite tacky. Test the surface with your finger first to check that it is not too wet. Once done, soften the effect a little with a softening or stippling brush. This effect also works well on its own.

# DÉCOUPAGE

DÉCOUPAGE is one of the simplest, most effective, and cheapest of the decorative finishes, successful on many types of furniture. You can do a découpage on any surface, as long as it is clean enough for the glue to stick well. Various materials are usable, including snippets from magazines, newspapers, photographs, greetings cards, gold and silver paper, and pressed flowers. The wider the range of colours and subject matter, the better. There are découpage books available which contain a variety of designs that can be coloured with watercolours or pencils, if you wish. It is important to test the scraps with varnish, in order to see if the paper is too porous; some thin paper allows the picture on the reverse side to show through, so thin pictures should be sealed.

As you begin to make your design, cut neat edges and place the cut-outs edge to edge, trying not to overlap them. Apply the glue sparingly to prevent the surface bubbling, using a small artist's brush to glue down narrow strips. Allow the surface to dry out completely before you start applying polyurethane varnish.

Use a varnishing brush or a small household brush. If you build up two to five coats of varnish over a few days, allowing each layer to dry completely, the surface will last for years. Between each layer, rub down the surface very lightly with fine wire wool.

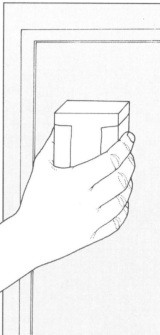

◀ *Prepare your surface by cleaning it well and filling any holes or scratches. Next, paint it with eggshell or emulsion and drag or rag it if you choose. Apply sealer, and once dry, sand it gently with some fine sandpaper to make it smooth enough for the glue and paper to stick well.*

▶ *Holding the picture in your left hand, cut out the paper scrap neatly by turning the paper rather than the scissors, always cutting out from underneath the paper upwards. A sharp craft knife is sometimes better for very intricate areas. Arrange the scraps edge to edge on a piece of paper the same size as the object you are going to decorate, and rearrange until the design suits.*

---

**MATERIALS**
- Suitable scraps
- Sharp scissors (small and large pairs)
- Glue or paste
- Roller
- Sealer
- Polyurethane varnish
- Varnishing brush or household brush
- Artist's brush
- Damp towelling cloth
- Sponge
- Fine sandpaper
- Fine wire wool

▶ Leave the découpage to dry completely (preferably overnight). With a varnishing brush, apply up to five coats of polyurethane varnish over several days to achieve a hard-wearing finish. Allow each coat to dry for about 24 hours, then rub down lightly with fine sandpaper before applying the next coat.

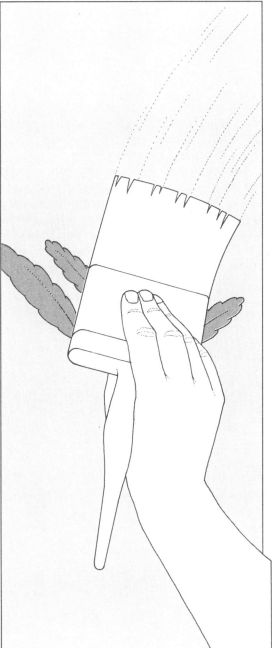

▲ Transfer the scraps to your chosen surface, one at a time, and stick them down carefully, using a small artist's brush to get the glue underneath edges and into difficult corners.

▶ Cover with a damp towelling cloth, and apply the roller over the surface. Use a slightly damp sponge to remove any excess glue; work from the centre outwards.

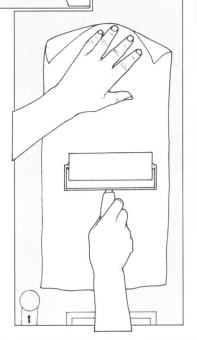

# PRINTING

PRINTING is one of the simplest and cheapest techniques, and can be done on plain or variously-decorated surfaces. Shapes can be cut out of wood, vegetables, sponges and all sorts of found objects. Printing works well on most hard surfaces, although the quality will depend on the absorbency of the surface, the paint, and the type of printing block you use. For border patterns, repeating one motif is simple and quick to do, and rewarding, too.

One of the easiest methods is to cut a simple shape out of a synthetic sponge. The sponge allows you to print over uneven surfaces. On a flat, smooth surface, a wooden block works better. For ease of use, screw a small wooden handle into the back. Cut-out flat shapes made from card, cork tile or polystyrene, for example, can then be stuck on.

Alternatively, good prints can be made from vegetables such as potatoes, turnips and swedes if cut in half and used with ready-mixed water-based paints. Either brush the paint on to its surface, or wipe a little on a paint tray and stamp the vegetable on to it. It may be helpful to stick a fork into the back of the vegetable to serve as a temporary handle. Vegetables take a while to absorb the paint, and the quality of the print will improve as you use it. It is a good idea to experiment on paper or card before you start printing on furniture, although the beauty of prints lies in their erratic nature and often incomplete effects.

One of the easiest choices for printing is childrens' ready-mixed PVA paint, although oils, acrylics and all household paints work well. Vegetables print best with water-based paints; oil paint does not mix well with the water in the vegetables, although it does adhere to the surface. Water-based paints dry more quickly than oil-based ones, and you will need to apply them more frequently, but you can really use whichever paint you prefer. I happen to prefer using oils, but many people find them messy.

---

**MATERIALS**

- ♦ Ready-mixed PVA, oil- or water-based paint
- ♦ Suitable materials for printing (vegetables, sponge, wooden blocks, corks, bottle tops, cotton reels, polystyrene, plastic cups, etc)
- ♦ Household brush
- ♦ Paint tray
- ♦ Clean cotton rag

---

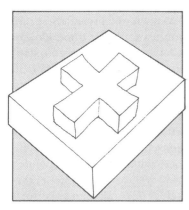

◀ Make the printing block by cutting a shape out of a vegetable, sponge, wooden block or other object suitable for the surface.

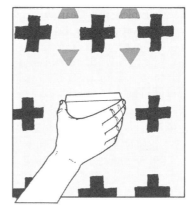

◀ Press the block over the surface, taking care to print neatly. If you are going to print an overall pattern, it is a good idea to mark occasional guide-lines with chalk.

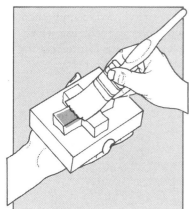

◀ Either brush the ready-mixed paint on to the block with a household brush, or dip the block into a small amount of paint on a tray.

◀ More than one block can be used to add interest. If using one on top of the other, allow each coat to dry in-between to prevent colours merging undesir-ably. Wipe the blocks clean with a rag if using different colours.

# STENCILLING

STENCILS are easy to make from acetate and stencil paper, and there is a wide range of ready-made stencils available to buy. They can be based on almost any image, and need not be complicated; simple shapes work well, too. You may prefer to trace a picture, simplifying it if necessary, or even better, design your own.

Draw out your design first, keeping it simple, and incorporating bridges. These are the areas that will hold the stencil together, and are not cut out. They show up white on the surface, and form part of the design. Trace or redraw your design on to a stencil card or a piece of acetate, and cut it out with a sharp scalpel or craft knife. If you cut through a bridge, repair it with a little masking tape stuck on both sides of the stencil, trimmed to follow the shape of the design. Test the stencil on a piece of paper first to see how the design looks, by brushing some colour over it.

You may work on any basecoat, but perhaps the best one to use is eggshell, as this will enable you to wipe off your mistakes easily. If the furniture has been waxed you will need to remove this, using a wax cleaner. Then you can stencil straight on to the wood, and afterwards seal it with beeswax or a polyurethane varnish. Finishes such as ragging (see p.106) and colour-washing (see p.102) also make good bases for stencilling, since their effects complement the informal edging of the stencil.

You can choose from several methods to apply colour. An even, short-haired brush or a stencil crayon both produce a slightly grainy effect, and car spray paint gives a fine, delicate finish, with definite edges. With all stencilling, you need to be light-handed when applying the colour, building it up gradually. By using oil paints, mistakes can be rectified simply by wiping off with white spirit. Acrylics dry quickly and cannot always be removed successfully.

Try to keep the colours close in tone, otherwise the stencil will be too contrasting and the result will look crude. Only a little colour is required to create a pleasing effect, so put a very small amount of colour on the brush, and work in soft circular strokes, building up slowly until you have enough. Keep a separate brush for each colour, and as you work, gently merge the edges of the colours together. Small errors will not be noticeable on the final design.

---

**MATERIALS**

- ◆ Eggshell basecoat or emulsion
- ◆ Stencil paper or acetate
- ◆ Paint (quick-drying spray paints, oil or acrylic paints) or stencil crayon
- ◆ Cutting board
- ◆ Craft knife or scalpel
- ◆ Stencil brushes
- ◆ Masking tape and adhesive
- ◆ White spirit
- ◆ Paper, pencil and fibre-tipped pen

---

▼ *Draw the design of your choice, allowing for bridges between the shapes. These will not be cut out, as they serve to hold the stencil together. Shade in the areas to be cut out so that you can check that the bridges are sufficiently sturdy and in the correct position.*

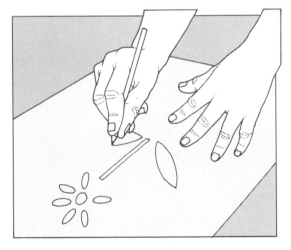

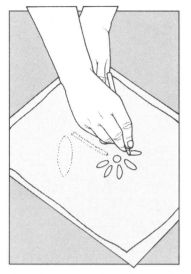

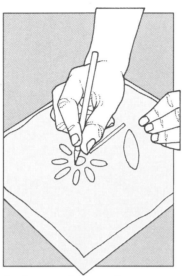

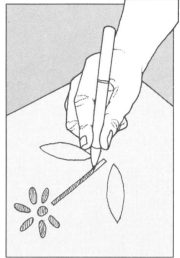

▲ *Make a tracing of your design and use this to transfer it on to the stencil card, or, if you prefer, trace it directly on to a sheet of acetate.*

▲ *If using card, reverse the tracing paper on top of a piece of manilla and scribble over it with a soft pencil to transfer the design.*

▲ *Using a felt- or fibre-tipped pen, shade in the areas that are to be cut out to avoid making mistakes later on.*

▲ *Cut out the stencil with a craft knife or scalpel, pulling the knife towards you, and turning the stencil paper rather than the knife.*

▲ *Cut out registration marks in the corners of the stencil card, to help you to position it later, then test it with some colour on a piece of paper.*

▲ *Apply the colour very lightly, with only a little paint on the brush. Use a dabbing and brushing motion, adding colours a little at a time.*

▲ *If using spray paints, attach your stencil to the surface with adhesive, and mask off the surrounding areas with masking tape.*

▶ *Apply your colours with a light hand, building up the effect slowly. The colours can be mixed together on the surface by spraying one on top of another. Use spare pieces of card as guides to direct the area of the spray.*

## WHEN USING SPRAY PAINTS

◆ *Check that the spray paints are free of chloro-fluorocarbons; these chemicals are damaging to the ozone layer.*
◆ *Always work with one or two windows open to allow ventilation in the room.*
◆ *If possible, also wear a protective mask, available at car spray-paint shops.*
◆ *Always shake the spray can well before use, and when finished, turn it upside-down and clear the nozzle of paint by spraying it a few times on to some newspaper.*
◆ *If the nozzle becomes clogged and sticky, swap it with one from another can.*

## STENCILLING WITH FOUND OBJECTS

Almost any flat object may be used as a stencil, and can be either something solid, such as a leaf, or with cut out shapes, for example, a paper doily. This is one of the easiest and most satisfying objects to use, as it creates lovely star and flower patterns which you can repeat as often as you like. Paper doilies work best when used with spray paint rather than brushes, because

they are flimsy and break easily, and the spray paint is light and fine. You have to use the spray paint gently since only a little colour is needed to give a good finish.

Another suitable material, which can create really beautiful stencils is lace. A Victorian decorating book mentions a New York gentleman who suggested making stencils out of cut up lengths of lace curtain. His idea was to attach a piece of lace to a wooden frame, possibly in a square frame like a tapestry. The next step would be to coat the lace with a layer of shellac, which is a resinous varnish that hardens the lace as it dries. Once dry and hard, the piece of lace would be removed from the frame and could then be used as a stencil, producing a very delicate image.

If this idea appeals to you, a modern adaptation of the idea is to use pieces of net curtain instead of lace, which can be cut up to whatever size and shape you require. The piece of net curtain is then dipped into a bowl of dilute varnish and hung up to dry. It is then ready for use as a stencil.

# CRACKLURE

THE TERM cracklure applies to two types of cracked paint. The first is achieved by applying two types of varnish (cracking and ageing varnishes), each with a different drying time. You can produce a cracked surface as the chemicals in the two varnishes work against each other. The surface must be non-porous or sealed first, because if the first layer of varnish sinks in, no cracks will appear. The effect is like old porcelain.

Apply the ageing varnish first, let it begin to dry, and while it is still sticky, apply the cracking varnish. Cracks will begin to appear on the surface. The longer the time lapse between varnishes, the smaller the cracks will be. If the cracks are too small because the first coat was left too long, wipe the second coat off with a white spirit-dampened sponge and repeat the process, leaving it to dry for less time.

To accentuate the cracked effect, apply a mixture of oil colour and clear glaze to the cracks with an artist's brush, using a contrasting or matching tone, and rub it over with a clean cotton rag to remove any excess. Seal the surface with one coat of polyurethane varnish. The second effect is achieved by using two coats of emulsion paint with a sandwich of a clear glaze which has a different repelling effect on the second coat. The final effect looks like old peeled paint. This can be either waxed or varnished afterwards.

---

**MATERIALS**
- Cracking varnish
- Ageing varnish
- Oil colour (amount to suit)
- Clear glaze
- Varnishing brushes
- Clean cotton rag
- Small artist's brush
- Polyurethane varnish

---

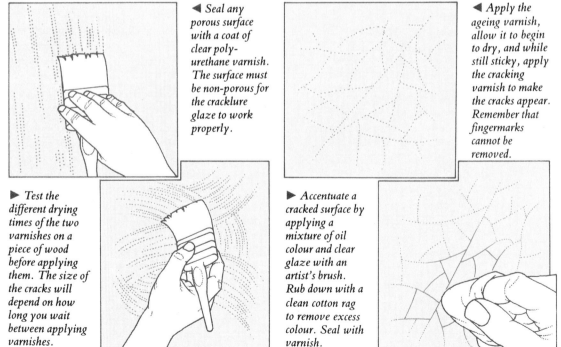

◀ *Seal any porous surface with a coat of clear poly-urethane varnish. The surface must be non-porous for the cracklure glaze to work properly.*

◀ *Apply the ageing varnish, allow it to begin to dry, and while still sticky, apply the cracking varnish to make the cracks appear. Remember that fingermarks cannot be removed.*

▶ *Test the different drying times of the two varnishes on a piece of wood before applying them. The size of the cracks will depend on how long you wait between applying varnishes.*

▶ *Accentuate a cracked surface by applying a mixture of oil colour and clear glaze with an artist's brush. Rub down with a clean cotton rag to remove excess colour. Seal with varnish.*

# DISTRESSING

DISTRESSING is the art of imitating the various signs of wear and tear that together give wooden furniture its characteristics of age, such as dents, scratches worn-away paint and varnish, and woodworm holes.

To give an aged look to furniture that is already painted, begin by covering it with a coat of polyurethane varnish and allow it to dry completely. The furniture can then be distressed without damaging the wood underneath the layers of paint. Coarse wire wool or a round-headed hammer can also be used gently to blunt the corners and edges.

Scratchings or scarring is rather more drastic. However, you can easily scar a flat surface by striking it with a bunch of keys threaded on to the handle of a coat hanger. More dramatically, you can drop a brick on to the surface from a height of two to three feet, taking care not to

miss your target and damage your feet instead.

In addition to blunting and scarring, woodworm holes can be reproduced, using suitable nails or an ice-pick, hammered into the wood. Study the formation of real woodworm holes carefully before attempting to copy them.

Having thus acquired the beginning of an aged appearance, your furniture is ready for the next stage. Using your finger, rub a little thinned oil colour into the scratches that you have made; Raw Umber looks most authentic. Alternatively, rub in a dark brown wax over a water-based paint which has been sandpapered to reveal either the plain wood underneath or another layer of paint. Allow this to dry thoroughly, then apply one or more layers of polyurethane varnish, "dirtied" with a little Raw Umber, allowing each coat to dry completely before applying the next.

**MATERIALS**
- Oil colour: Raw Umber
- White spirit
- Coarse wire wool
- Round-headed hammer
- Cotton rag
- Bunch of keys, coat hanger, nails, ice-pick
- Polyurethane varnish

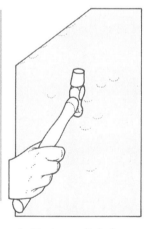

▲ *Having applied a layer of polyurethane varnish and allowed it to dry, rub down the corners and edges with coarse wire wool. Use a round-headed hammer for blunting corners, and dent the surface by tapping it gently.*

▲ *To "scar" the furniture, thread a bunch of keys on to a coat hanger, and, holding one end of the hanger firmly, strike the surface. Woodworm holes can also be simulated using an ice-pick or nails tapped into the wood in appropriate places.*

▲ *Using your finger, rub a little thinned Raw Umber oil colour into the scratches. Remove any excess with a rag. Allow to dry, then cover the surface with a coat of polyurethane varnish with a little Raw Umber added to "dirty" it.*

# USEFUL ADDRESSES

I would like to thank Robert Moss, for helping to prepare the furniture; Claire Ansell and David Manuel, for helping to keep body and soul together; Sue Hawker, for lending me her chair to decorate; and Bret and Ray for finding pieces of furniture.

**DORLING KINDERSLEY would like to thank:**
ROB SHONE, for the line drawings; LORRAINE HARRISON, for the watercolour illustrations; FELICITY BRYAN, for allowing us to photograph some furniture in her home; THE SLEEPING COMPANY, 65, Wigmore Street, London W1H 9LG (tel: 01 486 3150), for lending the satin frill bed-linen featured on p.77; THE COVENT GARDEN GENERAL STORE, 111 Long Acre, London WC2 (tel: 01 240 0331), for lending the rugs featured on p.27 and p.43; ANDREW FARMER, E. Ploton (Sundries) Ltd, for providing specialist materials for some of the photographs; and J. RATCLIFFE & CO, (Paints) Ltd, Southport, for invaluable advice.

Most of these suppliers stock either preparation materials, wax gilt or glaze, but a few stock all the specialist equipment that you may need. In addition, they are able to order for you any items that they do not stock.

**BANBURY**
Milners of Banbury,
Waterside,
Lower Cherwell Street,
Banbury, Oxon OX16 8AY
0295 4209

**BATH**
H.W. Davies & Sons (Bath) Ltd,
19A Monmouth Place,
Bath, Avon BA1 2AY
0225 23749

**BELFAST**
Thomas Kelly & Co
(Paints & papers) Ltd,
44-48 Dublin Road,
Belfast,
N. Ireland
0232 320114

**BIRMINGHAM**
W. Habberley Meadows Ltd,
5 Saxon Way,
Chelmsley Wood,
Birmingham B37 5AY
021 770 2905 or 0103
(transfer and loose
gold leaf)

**BLACKPOOL**
Decorative Materials (Fylde) Ltd,
277 Church Street,
Blackpool FY1 3PB
0253 22123

**BOURNEMOUTH**
Hurst Decorating Supplies,
396 Holdenhurst Road,
Bournemouth BH8 8BN
0202 309351

**CARDIFF**
W.J. Gardner (Cardiff) Ltd,
131-141 Crewys Road,
Cathays, Cardiff CF2 4XR
Wales
0222 227631

**CAMBRIDGE**
Mcdougall Rose Group,
Cambridge Road Industrial
Estate, Milton CB4 4BA

**CHESTER**
Robinson & Neal Ltd,
19A King Street,
Chester CH1 2AP
0244 326551

**CLEVELAND**
W.H. Gibb & Sons Ltd,
292 Linthorpe Road,
Middlesbrough,
Cleveland, N. Yorks
0642 243045

**COLCHESTER**
Anglian Decorators Supplies Ltd,
Unit 12, Davey Close,
Greenstead Road, Colchester,
Essex
0206 870222

**DUNDEE**
G. & W. Henderson (Keyline),
Faraday Street,
Dundee, Scotland
0382 812621

**EXETER**
Joshua Rea & Sons Ltd,
7-9 Verney Street,
Exeter, Devon EX1 2AW
0392 76448

**GLASGOW**
Peter Fisher Ltd,
16 Trongate,
Glasgow G15 EQ Scotland
041 552 0913

**HULL**
Arthur Westerby & Co Ltd,
124 Boulevard, Hull HU3 2UE
0482 223513

**LONDON**
E. Ploton (Sundries) Ltd,
273 Archway Road,
London N6 5AA
01 348 0315 or 2838

Cornelisson, L. & Son Ltd,
105 Great Russell Street,
London WC1B 3RY
01 636 1045

Green and Stone Ltd,
259 Kings Road, London SW3
01 352 0837

The Dover Bookshop,
18 Earlham Street,
London WC2
01 836 2111
(stencil designs & books)

**LEEDS**
Firth, Ray & Prosser Ltd,
Albion House,
24 Roundhay Road,
Leeds LS7 1BT
0532 440841

**LIVERPOOL**
Robinson & Neal Ltd,
135-137 Dale Street,
Liverpool L2 2JL
051 236 2144

**LYDD**
Liberon Waxes Ltd,
6 Park Street,
Lydd, Kent
0679 20107
(preparation and gilding
materials – mail orders
accepted)

**MANCHESTER**
Bennet's British Brushes Ltd,
607 Stretford Road,
Old Trafford Bar,
Manchester M16 0QJ
061 872 0452

**NORFOLK**
L.V.E. (Norfolk),
34 Yarmouth Road,
Thorpe, Norwich NR7 0EF
0603 34896

**NORTHAMPTON**
Northampton Decorating
Services Ltd,
135 Stimpson Avenue,
Northampton NN1 4JN
0604 232141

**NOTTINGHAM**
W. Robinson (Nottingham) Ltd,
Alfreton Road, Bobbersmill,
Nottingham NG7 5NL
0602 784 241

Bladon Designs,
Knutsford House,
Park Street, Bladon,
Oxford OX7 1RW
0993 812590 (Liming, Crackle
and Antiquing kits)

(Liming, Crackle and
Antiquing kits)

**SCARBOROUGH**
The Paint People Ltd,
20 Castle Road, Scarborough,
Yorkshire YO11 1XA
0723 360704

**SHEFFIELD**
R.J. Stokes & Co Ltd,
12 Moor Street,
Sheffield S3 7UQ
0742 737211

**SOUTHPORT**
J.H. Ratcliffe and Co.
(Paints) Ltd,
135A Linaker Street,
Southport PR8 5DF
0704 37999
(oil glaze specialists)

**WITNEY**
Relics,
35 Bridge Street,
Witney, Oxon OX8 6DA
0993 704611
(preparation and gilding
materials – mail orders
accepted)